Why we wrote this book together

As experts in policy and research, the staff of the National Council on Teacher Quality got the idea for this book because of how little information is out there to help future teachers make the best possible decision about where to get their preparation. A big part of our work is assessing teacher preparation programs and how well they prepare teacher candidates to walk into the classroom on <u>day one</u>, really, truly, absolutely ready to teach effectively. We rate teacher preparation programs primarily on their application of scientific research to guide what prospective teachers will learn, to the same degree that other professions do. Over 15 years of researching and rating programs have helped NCTQ to become the leading expert in the nation on steering future teachers on a path to teaching excellence.

We asked Dan Brown to help us write this book because not only is he a former teacher, he has more knowledge than anyone about what aspiring teachers heading to college don't know and what they need to know about their preparation. While running the organization Educators Rising, Dan met thousands of teenagers from across the country who were interested in teaching. He listened to their questions, their fears, and the aspects of teaching they anticipated most. Then Educators Rising collaborated with experts, colleges, teachers, and leaders to provide as much guidance and support as possible so those students' first steps of their teaching journeys could be as strong as possible. He is truly on fire to help the next generation of bright young people in America become effective change agents through teaching.

Finally, no book about the path to becoming a great teacher would be worth its salt if you didn't hear from lots of teachers. That's why we asked Teach Plus teachers to contribute their expertise and wisdom. As an organization of high-performing teachers who teach in high-need schools, Teach Plus frequently asks its teacher leaders what education issues are of the greatest concern to them. A top answer is better teacher preparation. Teach Plus teachers overwhelmingly report inadequate teacher preparation experiences in which they did not get everything they needed to be ready to succeed in the classroom on day one. They had to learn on the job. They wanted to help with this book so you can have what they did not.

Given this need for better preparation and its ability to tap the perspectives of thousands of great teachers across the country, Teach Plus was pleased to partner with NCTQ and Dan Brown to produce this book.

Together, we hope you find this book to be just what you were looking for!

Why teach?

I like the challenge. I call teaching the most challenging fun I have ever had.

I like the influence I have. I like winning kids over, even if it takes years after they leave my classroom. I shape young people.

I like the change. I never teach the same way from year to year. I aim to change at least 25 percent of both how I teach and the content I teach.

I like the autonomy. At first you need a lot of input and insight into your instructional practice, but as you mature as a teacher you become more and more independent.

– Middle school teacher from West Virginia,
Teach Plus Fellow, 19-year teaching veteran

Start Here to Become a Teacher: What to Know and Where to Go

About the Authors

National Council on Teacher Quality

The National Council on Teacher Quality (NCTQ) is an independent, nonprofit, and nonpartisan research and policy organization that works to improve education so that all children are taught by effective teachers and all teachers have the opportunity to become effective. It is the nation's only source of comparative data on the quality of teacher preparation programs, updated regularly as the *Teacher Prep Review*. These ratings can be viewed at www.pathtoteach.org.

Most staff members at NCTQ have experience as teachers. All believe that changes are overdue in not just the preparation but also the recruitment and retention of teachers. To do its work, NCTQ receives funding from private foundations and individuals committed to change in education.

Dan Brown

Dan Brown is a National Board Certified Teacher and the author of *The Great Expectations School: A Rookie Year in the New Blackboard Jungle.* From 2013 to 2017 he served as Co-Founder and Co-Director of Educators Rising, a national network of more than 45,000 teenagers exploring teaching as a career path.

Our Contributor, Teach Plus

The mission of Teach Plus is to empower excellent, experienced teachers to take leadership over key policy and practice issues that affect their students' success. Since 2009, Teach Plus has trained thousands of teacher leaders across the country who are driving policy changes and improving the instructional practices of teachers to create an education system driven by equity, access, and excellence for all students. www.teachplus.org

A Letter to My Younger Self

Dear Dina,

I see you sitting at your desk hovering over a pile of college brochures with that deer-in-headlights look on your face. I know: you want to be a teacher more than anything. You knew in sixth grade that teaching was your calling. You remember your teacher and how mean she was to her students. You knew then that something wasn't right. Teachers should empower kids, inspire them, and give them the tools to succeed and be proud of themselves.

I know that's what you're thinking. How? I know because I am — well, was — you.

Here I sit, 29 years into my teaching career, and as I look back at everything I've done I want to let you in on a few Must Dos and Please Don'ts.

Let's begin with those colleges you're trying to choose from. Dina, PAY ATTENTION TO THIS. It is not all apples and roses in the teacher education world. Unfortunately, there are many — way too many — programs where getting a degree in education is an easy A. There are too many programs that never show you how to reach struggling students or that fail to put you in front of real students until your final semester.

Instead of one of those, please do choose a program that has rigor, demands intensity and has the highest caliber of professors to lead you on your path to becoming a teacher. Choose a program that EXPECTS you to be gaining hands-on experience in a classroom from first semester, year one.

Dina, you're making a great choice. Teaching is important, impactful work — and it's never boring. But in order to be really good, please do your research when finding the college you want to attend. Make sure it is high-quality. Make sure it will equip you with the powerful teaching knowledge you'll need.

I wish I knew these things three decades ago.

And Dina... one last thing. You're going to love teaching. Trust me.

From,
Yourself (just a bit older and wiser)

Dina Rock is currently in her 29th year of teaching. She teaches 5th grade language arts and social studies in Cleveland, OH.

Chapter 1:
Why You Need this Book

So, you think you want to be a teacher? It's exciting to think about: the impact, the fulfillment, and the connections with students. You want to be a role model with the power to shape the future. That is excellent. The teaching profession needs you.

To accomplish your dreams, though, you need to not just become a teacher, but to become a skilled, effective one.

This book will put you on the right path to doing that.

Start Here to Become a Teacher is a different guide, the first of its kind. We know there are a lot of college books out there, but this guide will give you unique advice about teaching found nowhere else, including descriptions of the nation's best teacher preparation programs at the undergraduate level. By reading it, you're about to become a better equipped traveler on your journey to great teaching.

When browsing websites or reading course titles, it may look like teacher preparation programs in colleges are all pretty much alike. They aren't. We know — we've done the research.

This book will help you to be a smart college shopper who can tell a great program from a mediocre one. It will also connect you with hard-earned wisdom and knowledge from some of the best teachers in the profession today — people who just a few years ago were in exactly your position trying to choose the right college for themselves.

Unfortunately, many aspiring educators who have come before you basically had to guess which college would be the best fit to prepare them to be great teachers. Maybe the guide on the campus tour was super friendly. Maybe their friend was going there. Maybe it was the closest to home. With this book in your hand, you now have the power to factor in a critical consideration: *will this college prepare me to be good at my job?*

It's a little wild that this information isn't more widely known. After all, teaching is a huge profession; there are more teachers in America than the number of doctors and lawyers put together. The U.S. has more than 3.8 million teachers, and on average 100,000 brand new ones are hired every year.[1] Every community has a teaching workforce.

Profession	Number of jobs[a]
Teachers	3,800,000[b]
Doctors	666,490
Lawyers	628,370
Nurses	2,906,840
Electricians	631,080
Restaurant servers	2,584,220
Actors and actresses	43,470
Architects	122,160

a   U.S. Bureau of Labor Statistics. (2017, May). Occupational Employment Statistics: National Occupational Employment and Wage Estimates United States. Retrieved 26 October 2018 from https://www.bls.gov/oes/current/oes_nat.htm#29-0000

b   Taie, S., and Goldring, R. (2018). Characteristics of Public Elementary and Secondary School Teachers in the United States: Results From the 2015–16 National Teacher and Principal Survey First Look (NCES 2017-072rev). U.S. Department of Education. Washington, DC: National Center for Education Statistics. Retrieved 24 October 2018 from https://nces.ed.gov/pubsearch/pubsinfo.asp?pubid=2017072rev.

In addition to its massive size, the teaching profession is massively important. A body of research shows that of all the various aspects of schools, such as class size, the condition of the school building, and the money spent on them, it is the classroom teacher that matters the most.

So if our country is counting so much on so many teachers to be great, why has it been so ridiculously hard for future teachers to "comparison shop" wisely among teacher preparation programs?

Fortunately, times are changing. The National Council on Teacher Quality (NCTQ), with the help of the teachers you'll meet in the upcoming pages, spearheaded this book for a big reason: we want you to become your best teacher self. Our kids and our country need you to be skilled and well-prepared when you enter the classroom as a licensed teacher. Of course you'll improve every year, but we want to help you to start strong.

Why You Need a Guidebook to Teacher Prep Programs

No matter what profession one enters, the first year can be tough. However, we're tired of hearing horror stories from first-year teachers who weren't ready for the reality of teaching. No one wins in those scenarios. Somehow our country has gotten used to traumatic stories about rookie teachers that sound more like a bad fraternity hazing than the beginning of an empowering professional journey. Starting to teach doesn't have to be so painful, and picking a quality preparation program is one important key to avoiding the horror stories.

The good news is there are undergraduate colleges that do it right. Many teacher prep programs meet the real-life needs of aspiring teachers: a firm grounding in the subjects they want to teach, how best to teach those subjects, and lots of practice under the wings of great mentors. The programs featured in this guide understand this.

What this book will tell you — and what other college guidebooks won't — is how well a program will prepare you to succeed in your first few years as a classroom teacher. Teaching is highly complex work, and preparing new teachers for success is a challenge that not all colleges handle well.

Other college guidebooks will help you choose a college that fits your budget or meets your requirements for size and location but say almost nothing about the quality of your individual major, including the teaching major. This book will show you where to go to gain the knowledge and skills you need to become a great teacher. It incorporates ratings from the nation's only evaluation of undergraduate teacher preparation program quality — the annual *Teacher Prep Review* that NCTQ has been conducting since 2013. You can find all of those ratings for over 2,400 different programs at www.nctq.org/review/.

You don't need to throw away those other guidebooks, but be sure to keep this in mind. Many top institutions in this book aren't at the top of the U.S. News and World Report college rankings. Those general ratings just don't consider the quality of teacher training that this book examines.

You might assume that universities with outstanding science, math, law, or engineering programs would also have excellent teaching programs. Surprise! Some of the universities with the highest general reputations (and often the highest price tags) do not have high-quality teacher education programs. Meanwhile, other institutions without the well-known brands of big-name schools have quietly focused on developing superior teacher prep programs.

The size of a college or university can also be misleading. Small teacher prep programs might offer more personalized attention and more customizable options, but there is such a thing as too tiny. That's because smaller institutions may not be able to afford all the faculty needed to offer the full range of coursework someone should have to become a well-prepared teacher.

For example, a high school biology teacher needs a "methods course," which specifically focuses on how to teach biology, including the techniques needed to teach biology well. Smaller programs may only be able to offer a general methods course, intended for high school teachers of any subject. The aspiring biology teachers at those colleges miss out on the crucial learning about how to teach their specific subject to students — because teaching biology can be very, very different than teaching French or algebra. We'll help you steer clear of those kinds of programs that won't help you access the specialized skills and knowledge you need.

What does this book tell you that you can't find in a general guidebook for a college or university? Three characteristics specific to teaching:

1. **Which programs will deliver the fundamental skills, like how to teach reading.** For example, if you're planning on becoming an elementary teacher, there is nothing more important than knowing how to teach your students to read. Believe it or not, most teacher preparation programs in the United States are not currently providing this foundational knowledge! In this book, we will tell you about the ones that do and those that deliver other fundamental skills.

2. **Where you will get the highest quality opportunities to practice teaching.** Every college is required to provide prospective teachers with a chance to practice teaching in a real classroom with help from a mentor teacher. But many colleges are not able to make sure that your mentor teacher is a great teacher. What could be more important? You only want to be trained by the best, right? This book will guide you to the programs that do pay attention to the quality of your mentor.

3. **Wisdom from strong experienced teachers.** You'll hear from a lot of successful current teachers who will share useful advice and perspectives that they wish someone had told them when they first pondered entering teaching. Since they were in exactly your position not so long ago, you can learn from their successes and avoid their mistakes.

So You Think You Know What Teachers Do

As you approach the end of high school, you've now been sitting in classrooms for over a decade, watching your teachers. You've sat through their lessons, taken their tests, read their comments on your homework, and observed how they manage and discipline the class. You've taken field trips with teachers and participated in extracurricular activities they organized. Observing all these years, you probably think you know all about what teachers do. There's actually a fancy term for the thousands of hours you have spent on the student side of teacher-student dynamics: "apprenticeship of observation."[2]

Of course you have well-informed opinions about who among your teachers was really good and who wasn't. You could list the reasons why some teachers were rock stars: They cared. They seemed really passionate about what they taught and could inspire their students to care about it too. They could be really funny. They had a great way of explaining things. They knew their stuff. They didn't just lecture at students but found ways to involve the class.

Skillful teaching requires intensive study, practice, and reflection — more than being a genius or having a heart of gold. The truth is that you've seen just one side of teaching, the public front. The apprenticeship of observation doesn't include what's hidden from view, the behind-the-scenes strategy work of great teaching. A lot more goes into teaching than what's visible to students. Teachers' brains are buzzing, making hundreds of decisions each school day.[3] To do that at a high level, teachers have to rely on a deep toolkit of professional skills and knowledge for each decision they make and each interaction they have. What may appear in the moment like instinct or improvisation are actually purposeful teaching moves.

There's a lot of ground to cover. Understanding the full scope of a teacher's role is key, and many teachers told us that teaching is no joke when it comes to the amount of work involved.

Lisa Christensen, a sixth grade English and social studies teacher in California said, "I think the multiple layers of responsibilities that a teacher has was really surprising. Planning, grading, collaborating, classroom management, committees, and meeting with parents are all crammed into such a small amount of time."

Lauren Pfeffer Stuart, an English Language Arts teacher in Beverly Hills, CA agreed, saying, "The work is never 'done.' There is always more: whether it's polishing a lesson, planning for the next week, contacting parents, preparing project materials, collaborating with colleagues... You just need to pick a point at the end of the day and say, 'I'm done for now.'"

But there are benefits from all these layers. Teachers report being amazed by the amount of freedom and flexibility in the job. Christina Jusino, a 9th grade biology teacher from Lawrence, MA said, "I think most people assume that a school hands you a curriculum that lays out exactly what's supposed to happen in your classroom. However, teaching is so much more dynamic, and even the exact same lesson will look and feel different based on the person teaching it. Even in schools that are highly structured and follow a specific curriculum, there's a great deal of liberty in how you decide to deliver that content, the manner in which you modify it for your individual student needs, and in what way you showcase your personality through your lessons."

This freedom and space for creativity can cut both ways. Aaron Grossman, a Montana fifth grade teacher admitted new teachers could get overwhelmed. He said, "I thought my district would provide a curriculum. It did not." Pattie Davis, an eighth grade teacher in Denver had a similar "go it alone" start to her career, saying, "What surprised me the most about teaching when I started was how much the profession really had such a sink or swim mentality. I never met any mentor and other teachers were too busy trying to stay afloat themselves to aid me. I [had to] figure it out on my own."

Teaching has its share of constraints as well. Heather McCarthy, a 5th grade teacher in Buffalo commented on "the extent to which the school day is shaped by outside influences, such as bus schedules, funding for before- and after-school programs, union contracts, and extracurricular scheduling. It may sound like a great idea, or be best for some kids to change a school's start or end time, but there's so much that goes into it. Nothing about a school's schedule is as simple as you may think!"

Other teachers told us they were impressed by their students. Dan Cultra, a 6th grade English teacher in Illinois said, "I was surprised by the diverse backgrounds of my students. I thought all students would be the same. Haha. Not quite. I learned quickly that each student comes from a unique situation and this is a strength for a diverse classroom." Barry Saide, a K-8 administrator in New Jersey admitted to being startled by "how much of role classroom management plays, and how keen student eyes are. They notice everything, even if they don't say anything." And a Rhode Island high school teacher said, "Building relationships with students is more important than anything else. They will not want to work for you if they don't trust you and if you don't understand and respect where they are coming from."

Teachers were blown away that all the stories about the power and impact of a great teacher were actually true. Liz Fitzgerald, a 5th grade teacher in Durham, NC, said, "As strange as this sounds, my biggest surprise has been that really great teaching can actually change the world and that a teacher's sphere of influence is infinite. It's not just a cliché!" A Tennessee elementary teacher agreed, "[I never expected] that this passion to teach would almost overtake my life because I want my students to earn the golden ticket in life: an education!"

Positive experiences with students generate rocket fuel for teaching inspiration and motivation. The flip side is that bad days or negative interactions can leave you dejected and exhausted. These things will happen, but over time, skilled teachers learn to manage their emotional responses to this demanding job.

In sum, teaching is hard. Skilled teaching takes years of intentional work. Each day teachers tap into a long list of strategies and responsibilities. Great teachers understand their subject's content in depth, as well as child development, motivational techniques, classroom management, lesson planning, public speaking, problem solving, and ways to help children with special needs. Teachers need to learn how to think on their feet, diagnose the situation in real-time, and select smart next steps when students struggle to comprehend the lesson.

Being a teacher means becoming a mix of being an instructor, motivational speaker, activity planner, improvisational performer, and social worker. You can probably think of even more roles that teachers unofficially play. Some of these skills are learned over time, with experience. Learning as many new skills and trying out as many new strategies as possible before you enter your first classroom as a licensed teacher will put you in the best position to be hired and be successful immediately. It will also set you up for a more successful career.

Doing all of this well requires that future teachers find the best possible teacher preparation program. We are here to help.

A Day in the Life of a 3rd Grade Teacher
by Gwendolin Bandi

Monday morning

I try to get to school thirty-five minutes before the bell so I can set up my classroom, make some copies and touch base with my colleagues before my students arrive. When our bell rings at 7:55 a.m., all staff make a point to be visible in the hallway, welcoming students with a high five or a handshake or a hug. I can check in with my students and see how their weekend went and address any issues or concerns. It's very positive for our school culture.

The morning is one of my favorite times. We share stories and a meal together, genuinely building a relationship. As an educator of newcomer English Language Learners, I know that unstructured conversation is essential. I highly recommend taking time to build relationships with your students prior to starting the day's academics.

After morning announcements and attendance, I teach a ninety-minute block of math each day and then forty-five minutes of science three days a week. We start our math lesson with a "warm up," or quick activity where every student participates. Since my students have limited English proficiency, I assign some students to read the prompt together as partners, while for other students I read aloud the problem or we read it all together. I post words on the walls and students keep their own math vocabulary notebooks.

It is incredible to see my students translating for one another throughout the day. By fostering a strong sense of community in our room, I encourage my students to take risks with speaking and writing. These moments of translation and peer collaboration strengthen the relationships in our class.

We transition from the warm up to our "mini-lesson," in which I briefly and directly teach the students a skill before setting them loose on independent or group practice of that skill. Today the mini-lesson is about related number problems. Students share both their answers and their strategies. This provides ample opportunities for speaking among the whole group or with partners.

Following the mini lesson is an investigation rooted in a real-life context such as helping my dad calculate the perimeter of our new porch, or the cost of the wood, or the amount of ounces in six cups of milk for my mom's mashed potato recipe. Embedding the problem in a real-life context drastically increases student engagement. It's literally more real to all of us in these terms.

Then we transition to our small group and "center" work time, in which students rotate to stations around the classroom where they engage in different tasks. As I help my students with their varying levels of language proficiency and literacy, I also work on their understanding of the many concepts we teach them. I focus on giving my students more structure and practice with concepts and topics. Students track their progress and set goals for themselves as they work independently.

After finishing math block, we hold a "closing circle," which is an opportunity for students to share what they learned. They also can compliment a peer about something the person said or did.

Our school has completely transformed our science block recently with hands-on, exploratory learning. Although many of my students are not fluent in English, they have extensive content knowledge. I take an "asset-based approach" to my students, embracing who they are and what they can do, rather than defining them by what they currently lack. They are eager to share their knowledge and add to it during our science investigations. They ask questions and provide explanations using words and pictures and diagrams. As the year progresses, they begin to sound more and more like scientists.

Following our math and science blocks, we break for lunch and recess to let our minds unwind. Teachers are constantly on the go in classrooms and it does take a physical and mental toll. I take the time to re-energize so I can tackle my day with my afternoon cohort.

As a departmentalized teacher, I only teach math and science, so my homeroom rotates to my humanities-based colleague's classroom and I repeat the lesson with her homeroom students. Although it is the same lesson, it is a different group of students and therefore it is never really the same. It's fascinating to reflect on how the same content and instruction plays out differently, and I'm able to develop insights and discoveries that I can apply to future lessons.

At the last bell, we dismiss our students, but the day isn't quite over. Teachers touch base with colleagues or call parents. I stay after school at least long enough to prep my room for tomorrow's lessons, make copies, and add notes to my lesson plans. We always take something home, whether it is homework to check, tests to grade, activities to prepare, or our thoughts and worries about our students.

There isn't a night that I go home when I am not thinking how I can explain a concept differently to that one student who struggled, or how can I help the student who struggles to make friends, or how can I support the student who has experienced trauma. I often fall asleep thinking of ideas to try out tomorrow in class. Teaching is open-ended; there's always more you can do to help your students become their best selves.

Gwendolin Bandi teaches math and science to 3rd grade English language learners in Fall River Public Schools, MA. She has been teaching for seven years.

Chapter 2:
Myth Busting and Job Advice

Can you guess the top reason people become teachers?

a. They love school and cannot imagine spending their lives anywhere else.

b. They want to work with young people.

c. They want to have summers off.

d. They've always heard faculty meetings are fun and... sometimes even a bit wild.

If you picked *b*, you're right. Does this sound like you as well?

Of course a desire to work with students isn't the only reason people become teachers. Other reasons include believing in the value of education in society, wanting to shape the future, and being influenced by a great teacher.[4] Do any of these hit home?

For more than a decade, Australia-based researchers Helen Watt and Paul Richardson have led the groundbreaking "Factors Influencing Teaching Choice (FIT-C)" study, which has identified trends in thinking among future teachers in countries around the world. Not surprisingly, they discovered that the number-one motivator for successful future teachers, whom they refer to in research-speak as "classroom engaged careerists" and "highly engaged persisters," is their desire to work with young people.[5]

Watt's and Richardson's research shows the second-highest factor for these fired-up future teachers is perceived ability. It sounds simple, but successful future teachers believe they'll be great at the job. They have confidence in their skills and knowledge, and in their capacity to do the job well. They envision a realistic future in which they are awesome teachers.

See what "perceived ability" and "interest in working with young people" sounds like in the words of real Teach Plus teachers:

Do you have a strong desire to work with young people?

"The kids give me so much energy! There's not a single second of boredom when you're in a classroom surrounded by thirty children."

"I love it when their faces light up because they finally understand a concept that has been difficult for them to comprehend. They are so excited that now they *get it.*"

"When a student comes to me having difficulty but by the end of the year shows such confidence — that's the reason I teach."

Do you believe that you will be a good teacher?

"I make a difference in my students' lives."

"I love pushing kids beyond what they thought possible and helping them realize their true potential."

"I like the ability to be with young people and help them through a critical time of their lives where they are 'trying to find themselves' so to speak."

Do you believe that a good education is a path to good and productive life?

"I also know that children are our future and we need them to succeed. I believe education is the great leveler and all students should have access to great teachers and great schools."

"I want every child to have access to an excellent education because I believe that it is a right not a privilege. If education is the only true universal experience, there's a huge opportunity to change the world through excellent teaching."

"I always wanted to leave the world better than it was when I came into it, whatever that means, and education ultimately became the clearest pathway to do that."

As we discussed in Chapter 1, doing the daily strategic work of teaching is a lot more complex than what students often assume. After all, from the student side of the desk one can only observe the visible aspects of the job — not the behind-the-scenes strategy and professional knowledge that shapes every moment of teaching.

Teaching is one of the most rewarding jobs, but it is difficult to do it well. As a teacher, you're constantly connecting with students, thinking on your feet, and planning your next move. The bonds you form with your colleagues and students over the marathon of a school year are hard-earned and irreplaceable. Every day is an epic journey of successes, failures, and second chances with real students who are counting on you. Few folks who don't teach can truly understand the challenges and rewards of teaching, so they often go with the flow of disrespecting it, or make the common mistake that your paycheck is the full measure of your worth.

In this chapter, we'll provide a clear picture of the road to great teaching with the help of real teachers so that you can go forward with your eyes wide open.

Myths About Teaching: Responding to the Haters

There's no sugarcoating it — **teaching is hard.** But that challenge is probably attractive to you. After all, who wants to do a job that is always easy — and likely kind of boring?

Because teaching is hard and even disrespected by some, many students who express interest in it inevitably face discouragement from people close to them. This may include friends, family members, and other teachers.

Of course we encourage you to give thoughtful attention to all advice you receive. This section of the chapter is intended to provide you with useful information to take into account in case the discouragement you hear veers into commonly repeated myths.

"Teaching is easy. Try something more stimulating."

No! Teaching is one of the most complex jobs out there. Being a good teacher is challenging, satisfying work. Many former teachers say teaching was much harder than what they did for their subsequent careers, yet they felt they were making a more meaningful difference in people's lives while teaching.

The best armor against this diss on teachers is to actually try out teaching — tutor, work at a camp, create instructional YouTube videos! Get a feel for what it's like, and begin to understand for yourself the intellectual challenges and rewards. Your personal experience will be a truer guide for you as to whether teaching is too easy — or too hard.

"Those who can, do. Those who can't, teach."

Originally "He who can, does. He who cannot, teaches," this deathless jewel was vomited up by George Bernard Shaw in Maxims for Revolutionists in 1903. Other sections in the same text are titled Servants ("When domestic servants are treated as human beings it is not worthwhile to keep them...") and How to Beat Children. Thanks for everything, George Bernard Shaw. Let's look elsewhere for career advice.

"Teachers only work a few hours a day, and get half the year off."

They wish! American teachers work an average of 52 hours per week on job-related tasks, like prep time and grading papers, and, of course, classroom instruction.[6]

According to a survey of Teach Plus members for this book, they divide their work days, including time spent at home, as follows:

A Teacher's Day

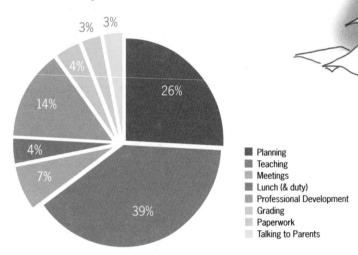

- Planning — 26%
- Teaching — 39%
- Meetings — 7%
- Lunch (& duty) — 4%
- Professional Development — 14%
- Grading — 4%
- Paperwork — 3%
- Talking to Parents — 3%

"Teachers make no money."

Teacher pay should be higher. They don't join the profession to become millionaires, but no one signs on for a vow of poverty either. In some really low paying states, like West Virginia, Oklahoma, Arizona, and Kentucky, massive protests and walkouts in the spring of 2018 brought national attention and modest raises. However, it is possible to live a successful middle class life on a teacher salary in many places. (We'll explore teacher pay in more depth in the next chapter.)

If the idea of teaching — spending your time and energy to help other people learn and grow — isn't inspiring to some people, that's okay. You're reading this book because it likely stirs something important in you. You're not alone; millions of educators across the country share that feeling. Having a meaningful job, where you never doubt the importance of your work, is incredibly important.

Many people join the private sector workforce and then switch careers to teaching because they want a job in which they know they're contributing something positive to the world. As a teacher, your work means everything to the students you see every day. What is bigger or better than shaping the future with a classroom full of unique young people?

And the work is exciting. Teachers are always on. You can't hide behind a computer or slack off, expecting someone else to step in and handle things for you. It's on you.

Ultimately, the path to being more informed than the naysayers is to test-drive teaching for yourself. You can find out if teaching is right for you by seizing every opportunity right now to start exploring it. This might involve asking to shadow teachers (they will pretty much always say yes and be delighted to host you), taking teaching courses, and signing up for clubs, summer programs, and mentoring opportunities where you get to teach.

If these types of programs aren't available at your school, you can be proactive and let your teachers, counselors, and administrators know about your interest in potentially joining their ranks. They can likely help set up individual opportunities for you to explore and try out teaching.

Finding a Teaching Job

The good news overall is that America needs teachers and is hiring, to the tune of about 100,000 new teachers on average in a year. In just the past four years, the number of teachers has expanded by 400,000 new positions.[7] The prospects also look good. According to census projections, the number of school age children (ages 5 to 17) will rise over the next 40 years so a lot more teachers will be needed.[8] You can be among them.

Population Projections (in thousands) Age 5-17

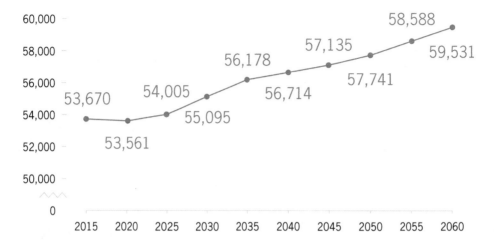

Unlike many careers whose jobs are located in specific areas (it's hard to be a lobsterman in Arizona), teachers work in every community in America.

Actually getting hired as a teacher can be a little confusing. You work every day in a school, but your paycheck comes from the school district. It's the district that manages the human resources processes and paperwork, and getting hired as a teacher means that the district is your employer.

School district websites have information about local processes for being hired as a teacher. These processes vary by district, but for one example, check out teachnyc.net for a clear description of how New York City Public Schools, the largest school district in the country, hires new teachers. Here are some of the materials candidates in New York City need to submit in their applications to the district to become teachers:[9]

- Professional background and resumé
- Academic history
- Professional references (typically 2-3)
- Sample lesson plan
- Responses to writing prompts
- Teacher certification for your state, or proof that you are on track to receive state certification before the new school year begins

The U.S. has around 14,000 school districts, and they vary hugely in size.[10] One school district includes an entire state (Hawaii) and the number of districts in Nevada (18) and Delaware (19) can be counted on one's fingers and toes. By contrast, Texas has over 1,000 districts!

Number of Districts per State

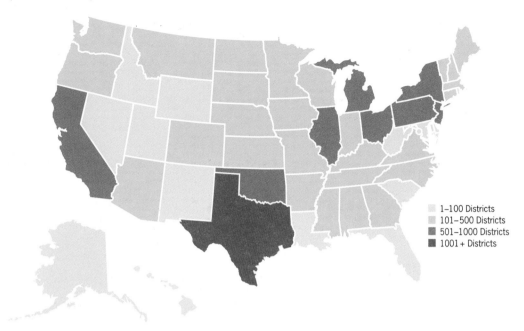

1–100 Districts
101–500 Districts
501–1000 Districts
1001 + Districts

Larger public school districts tend to have advantages for teachers as they may have dozens or even hundreds of schools, making it easy for teachers to have a range of opportunities and to transfer to another school within the district if desired. A smaller district may have just a couple of middle and high schools, or possibly even just one, so a laid off or unhappy teacher will need to find a job in another district. Generally, most new openings in larger districts are located in the most challenging schools, as many teachers frequently transfer out of the more challenging schools once they gain seniority. (A silver lining is that you can consider this trend an opportunity for you as a new teacher to have an impact with students who need support.)

In addition to traditional public school districts, over 200,000 teachers work in public charter schools, and those numbers continue to grow. Charter schools are public schools — funded by taxpayer dollars and tuition free — but they are allowed to operate under some different rules than traditional district public schools. Some states have a lot more charter schools than others. There are none in Alabama and North Dakota, but over 1,200 in California (9 percent of all public school students) and 700 in Texas (5 percent of all students).[11] In Washington, DC, more than two in five students attend a charter school.[12]

The U.S. also has nearly 35,000 private schools, and they employ nearly 500,000 teachers. Those are tiny numbers compared to more than 90,000 public schools (including charters), which employ more than 3.8 million teachers.[13] Most private schools have some type of religious orientation, with Catholic schools being the most prevalent. Non-religious private schools include Montessori programs, those that serve children in special education, or other alternative programs for children who may not get what they need from the local public school.

Here's an interesting fact. The majority of private schools (63 percent) are exclusively elementary, with more students enrolled in private kindergarten than any other grade. Private schools are typically small; half of them enroll fewer than 50 students. The average student to teacher ratio is 12 students per teacher, quite a bit different than the teacher ratio in public schools, which is estimated at 16 students for every teacher.[14] Far from being just a suburban phenomenon, there are just as many private schools to be found in big cities and small towns.

Choose your subject wisely

The need for great teaching candidates is especially high in certain subject areas. These include math, science, special education, and English language learners. If you are interested in specializing in any of these areas in which schools face chronic shortages, you have a great chance of being hired and even having schools compete for you.

Other subject areas like elementary school teaching or high school English have more candidates and more competition, but there is always a need for skilled teachers. If you can distinguish yourself as a talented and well-prepared new teacher, you have a great shot at earning a good job.

In states or regions where the job market is pretty competitive, you can increase your marketability by also earning a specialization in an understaffed area. For example, if you want to become an elementary teacher in New York, where there are many elementary teacher candidates, you might consider earning a specialization that allows you to also teach children who are learning English or perhaps a specialization in reading.

We encourage you to choose a preparation program in college that will provide substantial time — starting freshman year — for you to visit real classrooms and sample a variety of teaching subjects, age ranges, and types of schools so you can pick a specialization that matches your skills and fires up your passion. Build yourself into the most skilled, passionate young teacher you can be, and we're confident you'll find a school that will welcome you.

Teachers will be replaced with technology

No, they won't. Teachers are relatively protected from massive job losses due to outsourcing or technology because teachers have irreplaceably human roles that include mentoring, socializing, motivating, and encouraging students.

Technology may supplement teaching, but, at least in schools, machines cannot yet substitute for humanity. Experiments at some charter schools in hiring fewer teachers and putting students on computer terminals for large amounts of the day have not shown any promise that this model will spread significantly. Rosie the Robot won't be taking your teaching job any time soon.

There's a particular need for minority and male teachers

Many districts are actively seeking to build teaching workforces that reflect the demographics of their communities. Nationally, approximately half of public school students are white, while the teaching workforce is 82 percent white.[15] Increasing the number of skilled teachers of color is essential.

Similarly, fewer than a quarter of teachers are men.[16]

Teaching is not for everyone

Every profession has its downsides, and studies show teachers are no more likely to quit than those in other careers. The rate at which teachers leave the profession is far less than many people assume. People may tell you horror stories about half of teachers quitting in their first five years, but that figure is based on old research that has been disproven. Actually, more than four out of five new teachers stay with it. Among new teachers, a recent study found that only 17 percent of teachers — not 50 percent! — were no longer teaching four years later.[17] However, it's good to keep in mind that the rate of 17 percent is an average across all types of schools. Some schools in the heart of big cities or in rural areas struggle a lot more to keep their teachers.

Also, this study only looked at new teachers. About eight percent of the total teacher workforce leaves in a given year. Of that group, a little more than a third are retiring after a long career and another third are taking another school system job. Many of the others leave but decide to come back later. The fraction who leave <u>permanently</u> because they are unhappy is pretty small. So if you become a teacher, there is a good chance you will be starting on a long professional path in education, or one to which you may return after you take a break.

You can change your career

Choosing to become a teacher does not chain you permanently to the field if you realize it isn't a good fit or if you decide you want to try something new. Teaching builds many transferable skills in leadership, project management, group facilitation, and team dynamics. All of these can prepare you for other paths in life.

You would not be alone. About a third of former teachers move at some point to new roles in the education system. Most principals and other school and district administrators started out as classroom teachers. Former teachers also become staff members at state and federal departments of education, colleges, and in nonprofit or community-based organizations working on education issues. Almost all of the staff at NCTQ are former teachers! Others may work in children's programs, educational publishing and testing, museums, or historical sites.

Outside of education, former teachers become lawyers, entrepreneurs, doctors, nurses, salespeople, social workers, and managers.[18] Teaching skills also can be helpful for activity directors, trainers, human resources leaders, counselors, therapists, life coaches, and any job that values connecting with others, communicating, and helping people.

So, even if you change your mind about teaching, your years in the classroom — and your teaching degree — will be useful stepping stones for a new professional journey. Even when former teachers leave education completely, they can demonstrate to potential employers how their teaching experience can help them in a variety of careers.

Three Famous People Who Once Taught

Lin-Manuel Miranda

Now celebrated worldwide for writing the music and lyrics for and starring in the Broadway hits *Hamilton* and *In the Heights*, Lin-Manuel Miranda started his professional career teaching seventh-grade English in New York City. His passion for history and literature shines through in his songs and shows, and apparently it did as an educator in his early twenties as well. Manuel remembers, "One of my two favorite things to teach was *Things Fall Apart* by Chinua Achebe. It was amazing to watch seventh graders grasp it because there is some really tough stuff in it, but once they got their heads around it, it inspired a lot of amazing writing from them. The other one was *A Midsummer Night's Dream*. The best way to teach any Shakespeare is to get up and do it because they're plays — they're not pieces of literature to be read — and so I'd make every kid in the class play a part every day, and we read through the whole play, and it was a lot of fun."[19]

Lyndon B. Johnson

The 36th President of the United States, Lyndon B. Johnson started his career teaching English language learners, mostly the children of Mexican-American farmers, in Cotulla, TX near the Mexico border.[20] He dedicated himself to his students, even using his own money to buy playground equipment. As president, he said, "I know that education is the only valid passport from poverty."[21] When President Johnson signed the Elementary and Secondary Education Act in 1965, emphasizing equal access to education and a law still in effect today, he was capping off his life's experience as a teacher and advocate for education. He reflected on the value of teaching, "If I had to start life over again I would feel now, as I did almost fifty years ago, that I would want to be either a teacher or a preacher or a politician. Because... you are dealing with humanity."[22]

J.K. Rowling

While teaching English for two years in the small city of Porto, Portugal, Joanne Rowling found inspiration and began writing *Harry Potter and the Sorcerer's Stone*. The black-caped school uniforms in Porto look a lot like Hogwarts robes, and a street where she used to write before teaching resembles Diagon Alley. Perhaps her teaching colleagues inspired the tough but empowering Professor Minerva McGonagall, or the dull and lazy Cuthbert Binns!

A Day in the Life of a High School English/Research Teacher
By Troy Bradbury

The day-to-day experience of teaching is both universal and unique. The teacher must create it, curate it, and see it through to completion.

Many skilled teachers are planners; they decide what they will do every day and adjust as needed. I am not a planner. That isn't to say I don't have a plan. I do. I know what I need to teach but I allow for improvisation, like a musician. I know the key I am in and I play off of a riff. Sometimes we play a song and sometimes we just jam. I rely on my experience so that this leads to learning and discovery, not random activities and chaos.

My schedule is part English and part AP Seminar and Research. Forty-five minutes at a time for six periods a day, we're focused on reading, writing, problem solving, media literacy, and research. I have to anticipate their questions, including the ones they don't know to ask.

My schedule is based on the *who, what, where, when, how*, and — most importantly — the *why* of my day. The *why* helps me articulate my decisions for everything I did.

Then I attend to the administrative tasks of being a teacher: grading, meetings, taking attendance, paperwork, professional development, etc. These are a part of what it means to be a teacher today.

I call my style of instruction "The Long Conversation." This conversation happens throughout the year with multiple topics, arguments, solutions, writings, readings, and presentations. I spend my day in *The Long Conversation* with students exploring global education, 21st century skills, nonfiction and fiction. I am developing the *confidence* and *competency* my students need in the world.

I'm constantly checking their understanding and growth in all kinds of ways. My focus and goals for the day change based on what happened the day before. Before I leave my classroom, I reflect on every class, lesson, and student interaction. I ask myself, What went well today? What didn't go well? What do I need to do tomorrow? How will I get there? What do my students need? These questions guide my planning.

Teaching and being a teacher are not the same thing. Teaching is magic. Being a teacher is hard.

The time I spend in my class with my students is the best part of my day. Some classes are better than others. Some days I am a better teacher than others. But every day I want to be there.

As Ice Cube once said, "Today was a good day."

Troy Bradbury teaches 9th and 12th grade English and AP Capstone: Seminar and Research at Eleanor Roosevelt High School in Prince George's County Public Schools in Maryland. He has taught for 18 years and is the AP Capstone program coordinator and the University of Maryland, College Park Professional Development School site coordinator.

Chapter 3:
The Best Way to Become a Teacher

It may feel like a long, long distance from where you are now to becoming an official teacher in charge of a real classroom. Let's walk together through all of the steps and choices in becoming a teacher. Your own journey is very much the same journey that millions of teachers have already taken. If they could do it, so can you.

Becoming a teacher obviously isn't as simple as visiting a school and asking the principal for a job. Public school teachers, who account for the vast majority of all teachers,[23] need to be *licensed* (also known as *certified*) by their state. In most states, traditional public schools can only hire teachers who have completed a teacher preparation program that the state has approved and who have passed certain tests.

As an aspiring public school teacher, you will need to decide what you want to teach so that you can earn a license in that specific field. A French teacher, for example, must earn a different license than a middle school social studies teachers or a first-grade teacher — which means taking different courses and different state tests. Normally you will only be allowed to teach the subject in which you are certified.

This system, in which teachers are required to specialize and then are hired for their specialization, makes sense. Since expertise in your subject (often referred to as your "content") is so important for good teaching, you don't want to take a job that falls outside your licensing area. Think about the times you may have had a math teacher lead your history class — it's usually not a good fit for anyone.

Enrolling in a teacher preparation program is the most important step towards becoming a teacher and will play a large role in your ability to get the job you want. You are most likely to get your first teaching position near (or even at) the site where you do your student teaching, so you might consider asking programs where their student teachers are most likely to be placed.[24] That's a good predictor of where you'll get an offer to teach.

Let's look at some national trends in the job market that can give you an idea of what types of teachers are most sought after. Keep in mind, though, every state has different conditions and needs.

Commonly reported teacher vacancies

- Middle and high school mathematics
- Middle and high school science, especially chemistry and physics
- Special education
- Teachers teaching English language learners
- Foreign language

Areas with more applicants than jobs

- Elementary
- Middle and high school English
- Middle and high school social studies
- Art and music teachers

How can you decide which license you want to earn? Exploring your passions, considering the job market, and gaining as much information as possible are all important because most colleges will require you to select a specialization quickly.

And it's not enough for you to decide, "I just want to teach elementary school." You may have to choose if you want to earn an *early childhood* license (often covering birth through third grade) or an *elementary* license (typically kindergarten through sixth grade).

Not all colleges and universities offer every kind of specialization or license. For example, if you live in Missouri, you have to decide between two different pathways to become an elementary school teacher. You could choose Missouri State University, which makes it easy by offering both early childhood and elementary education licenses. However, if your heart is set on attending a small school like Drury University, you should know ahead of time that it only offers a program aimed at earning an elementary license (which would mean you could not teach kindergarten, for example.)

Routes into Teaching

Majoring in education in college used to be the only way to become a teacher. A lot has changed in the past three decades and the options have expanded. In this section we describe the many different ways someone can now become a teacher, giving you the pros and cons, as well as average cost data, for each.

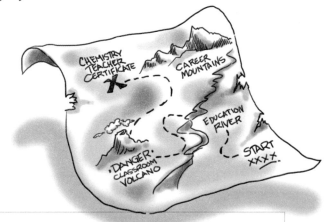

The many routes into teaching, circa 2018

TRADITIONAL UNDERGRADUATE FOUR-YEAR COLLEGE
Completing a four-year bachelor's degree at the same time as earning a license to teach.

Popularity: Most common route, roughly half of all teachers.[25]

Average Cost Per Year:	(Tuition, room, and board)
Public in state:	$20,770
Public out-of state:	$36,420
Private:	$46,950

The Good:	**The Bad:**
Getting licensed to teach while you are in college is one of the less expensive to become a teacher, since every teacher has to earn a college degree at some point. It also gets you into the school system at the earliest possible opportunity, so you can get started accumulating seniority and the pay increases that come with it. Finally, we find on average that undergraduate programs tend to be of higher quality than graduate or alternate route programs.	Not everyone realizes as an undergraduate that they want to be a teacher. Moreover, you should decide early in your program, so that you can enroll in the right courses (see Chapter 5 for more about this).

COMBINED TWO/FOUR YEAR COLLEGE
Community colleges usually only provide two-year degrees (associate's degrees) and cannot fully prepare their students to become teachers. However, many community colleges have programs designed for future teachers with the expectation that students will then transfer to a four-year school to finish their preparation.

Popularity:
About one in five education majors (22 percent) in undergraduate programs have already earned associate's degrees.[26]

Average Costs Per Year:[27]
(Tuition, room, and board)

2 years of community college (commuting) +
2 year of Public in-state: $12,170

2 years of community college (commuting) +
2 years of Private: $25,260

The Good:
Perhaps the least expensive way to become a teacher, as it leads to the same bachelor's degree that you would obtain from spending all four years at a four-year college. It also has the same benefits: getting you into the school system at the earliest possible opportunity and undergraduate programs tend to be better than graduate or alternate route programs.

The Bad:
While community college courses usually cost less, two-year institutions also typically offer less financial aid than four-year institutions. Be sure to do the math on tuition and fees to figure out the "true price." Many four-year institutions, especially private ones, will not accept some credits from community colleges. It's best to check with your intended four-year college ahead of time to see what they will count. Finally, take great care in following this route: just 14 percent of students who enrolled in community college earn a bachelor's degree in six years.[28]

GRADUATE SCHOOL
An aspiring teacher who already has a bachelor's degree enrolls in a graduate level program to earn a master's degree that includes a license to teach. Generally, the only courses you will take would be teaching courses. This type of program includes an unpaid student teaching experience, which distinguishes it from the alternative routes described below. The program can be completed in one year, sometimes two, depending on the requirements and the number of credits taken each semester.

Popularity:
A quarter of newly prepared teachers enter teaching this way.[29] Most California teachers have historically entered teaching via this route, since undergraduate routes directly into teaching in the state were banned until 2018.

Average Cost Per Year:
(Tuition only)
Public: $10,979
Private: $23,266[30]

The Good:
Nearly all districts pay higher salaries to teachers with master's degrees, generally about $2,000 to $4,000 more each year, starting in the first year of teaching.

The Bad:
Graduate programs in education often do not have enough time to teach the content that NCTQ sees as essential, such as the courses in elementary mathematics an aspiring elementary teacher likely needs or the subject area knowledge both elementary and secondary teachers required (see Chapter 5 for more about this).

ALTERNATIVE ROUTES

Aspiring teachers who already have a bachelor's degree can enter teaching through an alternative route in which they are "fast tracked," taking over a classroom as the full-time teacher at the same time they are learning how to teach. Teach For America is probably the best-known example of an alternative route program. Other alternative route programs may be run by school districts, universities, non-profit, or even for-profit organizations. Usually this route only provides a teaching certificate — no degree. Generally — but not always — programs require candidates to complete a few courses during the summer preceding the placement, with the bulk of the coursework completed while teaching during the academic year. You can learn more about the alternate routes in your state by going to https://www.nctq.org/yearbook/national?id=**438**.

Popularity:
About 20 percent of all new teachers, but it varies from state to state. Notably, nearly half of new teachers in Texas enter the profession through alternative routes.[31]

Average Cost:
Cost varies considerably for alternative route programs with some programs charging a candidate as little as $2,600 and as much as $63,000.[32] However, some well-known programs like Teach For America raise funds to reduce or even eliminate any costs to the candidate.

The Good:
Other than the undergraduate route, this can be the quickest way into the classroom regardless of what you majored in as an undergraduate.

The Bad:
The quality of preparation can be mixed and these routes require a strong mentoring and support component — which some just do not offer. Some for-profit providers need to be viewed with caution. As a result, some school districts are reluctant to hire teachers coming from an alternative route.

It can be very hard to take courses while teaching full-time for the first time.

RESIDENCIES

Residencies are only available to aspiring teachers who already have a bachelor's degree. They generally feature a year-long practice experience in a real classroom under the supervision of a veteran teacher. Resident teachers are paid a stipend (typically less than a full-time teacher salary). Resident teachers work with their peers as a cohort during evening and sometimes weekend coursework, often earning a master's degree.

Popularity:
Residencies are an increasingly popular option for aspiring teachers, with at least 80 programs available across the country. It's great for residents but expensive for school systems since teachers-in-training are being paid with stipends — rather than college students who are paying tuition for their training. As a result, residencies supply only about 1 percent of all new teachers each year.

Average Cost:
Would-be participants should ask questions until they are completely clear on the cost to participate, as these programs can cost up to $36,000 to the candidate, though the fact that you may earn a master's degree at the end should factor into your thinking. Some programs offer subsidized (someone else pays your tuition) master's degrees, while in others you have to take on the cost yourself.

The Good:
This is a great way to learn how to teach: significant hands-on learning before becoming the teacher of record, extensive support while teaching, and a pay check during it all.

The Bad:
These routes require a significant time commitment, typically four to five full-time days in the classroom plus an average of one full day of coursework per week, and may require a commitment to teach in the sponsoring district (generally two or three years after the apprenticeship ends). Finally, they may have too little critical coursework such as learning how to teach reading or elementary mathematics.

ONLINE

A number of for-profit companies and universities have created digital teacher preparation programs that satisfy the requirements for a teaching license. With few exceptions, most programs are graduate-level and not available to someone without a bachelor's degree.

Popularity:

Western Governors University, for example, offers online undergraduate and graduate courses in education and supports candidates in completing student teaching placements close to where they live. As of 2018, approximately 100,000 students have earned degrees in education at WGU.

Average Cost:

Varies significantly but almost always will be less than a campus-based program. The cost (tuition and fees) *per year* of a two-year online master's degree from Western Governors University is $6,603; from USC Rossier it is $27,026.

The Good:	The Bad:
Very appealing to career-changers, as the programs are typically flexible and let you proceed at a pace you can manage. They are typically very inexpensive, too.	Be cautious: many online programs are unaccredited, are often considered less rigorous, and may lack supervised practice opportunities.

NO FORMAL TRAINING

This option is only available to candidates who want to teach in schools that are not governed by statewide public education policies that mandate teacher licenses. It includes independent, private, some religiously affiliated schools, and some public charter schools. Few teachers in independent schools have teaching degrees. In fact, some independent schools view a teaching degree as a negative, seeking instead teachers who have spent extensive time specializing in their subject areas. Be aware that some states require even their religious and charter schools to employ certified teachers. You can check the website of your state education agency to find out what the rules are.

Popularity:

Private schools employ about 12 percent of the nation's teachers (approximately 400,000).

Average Cost:

None beyond the cost of a bachelor's degree.

The Good:	The Bad:
You might prefer to skip education coursework. Some private school jobs are more flexible on pay for performance and allow teachers to advance rapidly.	You receive no preparation in any of the essential skills in such areas as how to teach reading, managing a classroom, or working with more challenging populations.
	This route is not very marketable. Private schools offer far fewer jobs than do public schools. While private (often called "independent") non-religious schools tend to be more competitive on pay, private schools typically pay significantly less than public schools. Finally, if you start teaching in a private school and later switch to a public one, the public school might not count your private school teaching years as experience when calculating your new salary and will require you to be certified.

Availability of Loans

The United States has several federally funded programs to help teachers reduce or erase their student loans, and you should know about them as you plan your path to teaching.

Note that any information on student loans is subject to change, so be sure to get up-to-date information on these programs' official websites. Don't hesitate to reach out to those offices via phone or email with questions, and be persistent. Getting every little detail correct is a must when you're dealing with loans! Many teachers have horror stories about paperwork errors they made on their student loans that cost them thousands of dollars.

You'll want to spend some time on the Federal Student Aid website (studentaid.ed.gov) to learn more. Also the American Federation of Teachers has a helpful searchable database on its website (https://www.aft.org/funding-database) for "Loan Forgiveness & Funding Opportunities." You can also find funding opportunities through Teach.org at https://www.teach.org/scholarships-financial-aid.

If you're applying for a loan or grant that requires you to teach for a certain number of years, or in a certain subject or district, be sure to find out what happens — and what money you might owe — if you leave the classroom before your required time is up.

Federal Perkins Loans Cancellation

The federal government will cancel the Perkins Loans of **special education teachers**; **teachers of math, science, foreign language, bilingual education**, or **state-designated shortage area**; or **teachers in schools serving students from low-income families.**

See the Federal Student Aid website (https://studentaid.ed.gov/sa/repay-loans/forgiveness-cancellation/) for more information.

Loan Forgiveness — Low Income Schools

The federal government will forgive up to $17,500 of direct or Federal Family Education Loans to teachers who work in low-income schools. These schools are listed in the Annual Directory of Designated Low-Income Schools for Teacher Cancellation Benefits on www.tcli.ed.gov.

TEACH grants

Under a program called TEACH, the federal government will currently forgive up to $5,000 of loans for a highly qualified, full-time elementary or secondary school teacher. The amount increases up to $17,500 of loans for a highly qualified, full-time mathematics or science teacher in an eligible secondary school or a highly qualified special education teacher working with a population of children with disabilities that corresponds to the teacher's area of special education training. Visit the Federal Student Aid website listed above for more information.

Public Service Loan Forgiveness

Public and private teachers may also qualify for the Public Service Loan Forgiveness (PSLF) Program that forgives the balance of direct student loans after 10 years of on-time payments (120 qualifying payments) on an income-driven repayment plan while working full-time for a public service employer (including governments and tax-exempt nonprofits).

For all these programs, you should be aware that the U.S. Congress often threatens to reduce or eliminate their funding, so check the most updated information on the Federal Student Aid website.

Income-driven repayment

Most teachers qualify for an income-driven repayment plan, which puts a cap on your monthly payment (either 10 percent or 15 percent of your discretionary income) and then forgives the balance after twenty years. The four different versions of income-driven repayment options are explained in detail on the Federal Student Aid website (studentaid.ed.gov).

State loan programs

Your state may also have opportunities to reduce or eliminate your student loans. Check the teacher section of your state education agency's website.

Getting Admitted to an Undergraduate Teacher Preparation Program

Few aspiring teachers are admitted into a teacher preparation program right when they start college. You will most likely apply to a teacher preparation program at your school during your sophomore year of college. Unlike most other majors, many states have a distinct set of admissions standards for teacher preparation. That is because states must approve these college-based programs to essentially act as their agents, entrusting them with providing the preparation you need to become a licensed teacher in that state.

Here is the most current information available on the grades and academics you will need to gain admittance into a program, depending on the state you live in, and the state tests you will have to pass to get into a program. Keep in mind, programs will have other sorts of requirements for admission, but these are the grades and tests they require.

Start Here to Become a Teacher: What to Know and Where to Go

State	Do programs require you to have a certain GPA?*	Will I have to pass a test for admission into an undergraduate program?	What tests am I most likely to have to take to complete my preparation?**	
Alabama	Yes, 2.75	Yes	□ basic skills ■ elementary subjects ■ core secondary subjects	■ edTPA □ other pedagogy or performance assessment
Alaska	No	No	■ basic skills ■ elementary subjects ■ core secondary subjects	□ edTPA ■ other pedagogy or performance assessment
Arizona	No	No	□ basic skills ■ elementary subjects[a] ■ core secondary subjects[a]	□ edTPA ■ other pedagogy or performance assessment
Arkansas	No	No	■ basic skills ■ elementary subjects[a] ■ core secondary subjects	■ edTPA[g] ■ other pedagogy or performance assessment[g]
California	No	No	■ basic skills ■ elementary subjects ■ core secondary subjects[a]	■ edTPA[g] ■ other pedagogy or performance assessment[g]
Colorado	No	No	□ basic skills ■ elementary subjects ■ core secondary subjects[a]	□ edTPA □ other pedagogy or performance assessment
Connecticut	Yes, 2.7[b]	No	■ basic skills[c] ■ elementary subjects ■ core secondary subjects	■ edTPA □ other pedagogy or performance assessment
Delaware	Yes, 3.0[c]	Yes[b]	□ basic skills ■ elementary subjects ■ core secondary subjects	■ edTPA[g] ■ other pedagogy or performance assessment[g]
District of Columbia	No	No	■ basic skills ■ elementary subjects ■ core secondary subjects	□ edTPA □ other pedagogy or performance assessment
Florida	Yes, 2.5	Yes[c]	□ basic skills ■ elementary subjects ■ core secondary subjects	□ edTPA ■ other pedagogy or performance assessment
Georgia	Yes, 2.5	Yes[c]	□ basic skills ■ elementary subjects ■ core secondary subjects	■ edTPA □ other pedagogy or performance assessment
Hawaii	No	Yes[c]	□ basic skills ■ elementary subjects[a] ■ core secondary subjects[a]	■ edTPA[g] ■ other pedagogy or performance assessment[g]
Idaho	No	No	□ basic skills ■ elementary subjects ■ core secondary subjects	□ edTPA ■ other pedagogy or performance assessment
Illinois	No	No	■ basic skills[c] ■ elementary subjects ■ core secondary subjects	■ edTPA □ other pedagogy or performance assessment
Indiana	No	Yes[c]	□ basic skills ■ elementary subjects ■ core secondary subjects	□ edTPA ■ other pedagogy or performance assessment
Iowa	No	Yes	□ basic skills ■ elementary subjects[d] ■ core secondary subjects[d]	■ edTPA[g] ■ other pedagogy or performance assessment[g]
Kansas	No	No	□ basic skills ■ elementary subjects ■ core secondary subjects	□ edTPA ■ other pedagogy or performance assessment

* GPA requirements refer to early college coursework, not the GPA earned in high school.

** Does not include admissions tests. Elementary subjects are required only for elementary teachers. Secondary subjects are required only for secondary teachers.

a Can be waived by obtaining specific college degrees, sufficient course work credit, or work experience.

b Can be waived at program discretion or for meeting other criteria (such as GPA thresholds).

c Can be waived by adequate scores on other tests, such as the SAT or ACT

d You can take the content tests or the edTPA

e Required only for elementary teachers

f Required for social studies teachers only

g You can take the edTPA or another pedagogy or performance assessment.

State	Do programs require you to have a certain GPA?*	Will I have to pass a test for admission into an undergraduate program?	What tests am I most likely to have to take to complete my preparation?**				
			basic skills	elementary subjects	core secondary subjects	edTPA	other pedagogy or performance assessment
Kentucky	Yes, 2.75	Yes	□	■	■	□	■
Louisiana	Yes, 2.2	Yes[c]	□	■	■	□	■
Maine	No	No	■	■	■	□	■[e]
Maryland	No	No	■[c]	■	■	□	■
Massachusetts	No	No	■	■	■	□	■
Michigan	No	No	■	■	■[a]	□	□
Minnesota	No	No	■[c]	■	■	■	■
Mississippi	Yes, 2.75	Yes[c]	□	■	■	□	■
Missouri	No	Yes	□	■	■	□	■
Montana	No	No	□	■	■	□	□
Nebraska	Yes, 2.5	Yes	□	■	■	□	□
Nevada	No	No	■	■	■	□	■
New Hampshire	No	Yes[c]	□	■	■	□	□
New Jersey	Yes, 2.75	Yes[c]	□	■[b]	■[b]	■	□
New Mexico	No	No	■	■	■	□	■
New York	No	No	■	■	■	■	■
North Carolina	Yes, 2.7	Yes[c]	□	■	■	■[g]	■[g]
North Dakota	No	No	■	■	■	□	■

For additional detail, you can visit the NCTQ website at: (elementary) https://www.nctq.org/yearbook/national/Content-Knowledge-75
(secondary) https://www.nctq.org/yearbook/national/Secondary-Content-Knowledge-84

State	Do programs require you to have a certain GPA?*	Will I have to pass a test for admission into an undergraduate program?	What tests am I most likely to have to take to complete my preparation?**	
Ohio	No	No	☐ basic skills ☑ elementary subjects ☑ core secondary subjects	☐ edTPA ☑ other pedagogy or performance assessment
Oklahoma	Yesc	Yesc	☑ basic skillsb ☑ elementary subjects ☑ core secondary subjects	☐ edTPA ☑ other pedagogy or performance assessment
Oregon	No	No	☑ basic skills ☑ elementary subjects ☑ core secondary subjectsa	☑ edTPA ☐ other pedagogy or performance assessment
Pennsylvania	Yesc	Yesc	☐ basic skills ☑ elementary subjects ☑ core secondary subjects	☐ edTPA ☐ other pedagogy or performance assessment
Rhode Island	Yes, 2.75	Yesc	☐ basic skills ☑ elementary subjects ☑ core secondary subjects	☐ edTPA ☑ other pedagogy or performance assessment
South Carolina	Yes, 2.75	Yesc	☐ basic skills ☑ elementary subjects ☑ core secondary subjects	☐ edTPA ☑ other pedagogy or performance assessment
South Dakota	Yes, 2.6	No	☐ basic skills ☑ elementary subjects ☑ core secondary subjectsa	☐ edTPA ☐ other pedagogy or performance assessment
Tennessee	Yes, 2.75	Yesc	☐ basic skills ☑ elementary subjects ☑ core secondary subjects	☑ edTPA ☐ other pedagogy or performance assessment
Texas	Yes, 2.5c	Yesc	☐ basic skills ☑ elementary subjects ☑ core secondary subjects	☐ edTPA ☑ other pedagogy or performance assessment
Utah	Yes, 3.0	Yesc	☐ basic skills ☑ elementary subjects ☑ core secondary subjects	☐ edTPA ☑ other pedagogy or performance assessment
Vermont	No	No	☑ basic skills ☑ elementary subjects ☑ core secondary subjects	☐ edTPA ☐ other pedagogy or performance assessment
Virginia	No	Yesc	☑ basic skills ☑ elementary subjects ☑ core secondary subjects	☐ edTPA ☐ other pedagogy or performance assessment
Washington	No	Yesc	☐ basic skills ☑ elementary subjects ☑ core secondary subjects	☑ edTPA ☐ other pedagogy or performance assessment
West Virginia	Yes, 2.5	No	☐ basic skills ☑ elementary subjects ☑ core secondary subjects	☑ edTPAg ☑ other pedagogy or performance assessmentg
Wisconsin	Yes, 2.5	Yesc	☐ basic skills ☑ elementary subjects ☑ core secondary subjects	☑ edTPA ☐ other pedagogy or performance assessment
Wyoming	No	No	☐ basic skills ☑ elementary subjects ☑ core secondary subjectsf	☐ edTPA ☐ other pedagogy or performance assessment

* GPA requirements refer to early college coursework, not the GPA earned in high school.

** Does not include admissions tests. Elementary subjects are required only for elementary teachers. Secondary subjects are required only for secondary teachers.

a Can be waived by obtaining specific college degrees, sufficient course work credit, or work experience.

b Can be waived at program discretion or for meeting other criteria (such as GPA thresholds).

c Can be waived by adequate scores on other tests, such as the SAT or ACT

d You can take the content tests or the edTPA

e Required only for elementary teachers

f Required for social studies teachers only

g You can take the edTPA or another pedagogy or performance assessment.

Preparing in One State and Teaching in Another

Teacher preparation programs typically assume that the people in their program will end up teaching in that same state. Accordingly, they often prepare their candidates for that state's requirements. But there are a number of reasons why you may choose to enroll in an institution in one state and then teach in another. If you have the opportunity to attend one of the high-ranking programs in this book across state lines from where you plan to teach, that's a good reason. Even if you plan on moving to a different state after graduation, it may cost substantially less to pay in-state tuition at a public university in the state where you are living now. Other common reasons include wanting to stay close to home before moving to a state with higher teacher salaries, living near a border with another state (like DC, Maryland, and Virginia), or being recruited to teach in a state that offers incentives to lure talented out-of-state teachers.

However, since states determine their own policies for licensure, it can be a complicated, paperwork-heavy journey to prepare in one state and then teach in another. Exactly how many hoops you will have to jump through depends on the policies in the state where you want to teach. Many states don't trust the quality of each other's preparation programs, which can make this process notoriously difficult and bureaucratic. Persistence is necessary. You should count on having to contact the state education agency multiple times to get the answers you need. You may find it best to get a district interested in hiring you first so that it can help you make your case to the state. District staff may be more responsive, and because they know the ropes, they will be able to identify challenges or hurdles that the state is likely to raise.

Conclusion

If you want to be a good teacher right from the start of your career, your best move is to attend a high-quality teacher preparation program like those profiled in this book. Yes, some teachers succeed without it by spending their first few years learning on their own through trial and error. (Remember their students in those rough first years don't get a do-over on their education.) But those teachers who attend a high-quality program learn what research has proven to work, and they benefit from the experience of their instructors and cooperating teachers. As a result, their first few years of teaching are built on a strong foundation of knowledge, skills, and experience. The result is less stressful, and their students learn more.

Chapter 4:
Teacher Pay: Only Part of the Story

Teacher Pay and Benefits

When people sign up to become teachers, they are signing up for the impact they feel they can have on children's lives. That does not mean they are signing a vow of poverty. While teachers understand that the job won't make them millionaires, they can and should expect a stable, middle-class salary with benefits.

Since money is inevitably a factor in teachers' lives, it is important to examine the relative opportunities for pay and benefits compared to other professional paths. That's what this chapter does — and much of what we present here is likely to surprise you.

How much do teachers make?

So how much money will you earn as a teacher? This generally depends on:

- where you teach;
- how long you teach;
- how many degrees or advanced credits you have; and,
- in some places, what subject you teach.

Pay is seldom determined by how great you are as a teacher, but there are places that do recognize and compensate for talent. The most common way high performing teachers are rewarded is National Board Certification.[33] Approximately 110,000 teachers have become National Board Certified since the program was launched in the 1980s.

There are other efforts to provide great teachers with higher pay without teachers having to apply for that distinction, as is the case with the National Board, though none are as widespread. Dallas Independent School District and District of Columbia Public Schools in Washington, DC provide substantially higher salaries or bonuses to their most effective teachers, especially if those same teachers are willing to work in the toughest schools. Some great teachers with ten years' of service in Washington, DC are currently earning salaries over $130,000! In most school districts, however, it generally takes years for teachers to climb their way up their local "salary schedule," one step at a time, to earn top pay levels — longer than most other professionals.

Are teachers underpaid?

It depends on where you are looking as salaries vary a lot, but the short answer is yes. Teachers on average earn about 17 percent less than professions requiring the comparable level of education.[34] Increasing teacher pay is an important component of an ongoing national dialogue about improving education. (Check out the Teacher Salary Project for compelling videos and research on why and how to pay K-12 teachers more.)

That said, myths persist about just how poorly teachers are paid. Don't let urban legends scare you or your peers off. Let's take a look at the numbers, so you can make important life decisions based on facts.

> *People don't become teachers to become rich, and I always knew I wasn't driven by money. However, in my experience, the health care benefits have truly made up for low salaries. Knowing what my non-teacher friends have to pay out of pocket for healthcare benefits, I know my husband and I are taken care of well. Having built-in "vacations" and summer break is a definite plus, even though in my opinion I think most teachers are doing 12 months of work in 10 months, not to mention many teachers work over the summer anyway. Depending on where you teach, some schools or districts will pay for graduate classes, which is a plus, and there are certain federal loan forgiveness programs as well.*
>
> — *Heather McCarthy*
> *William A. Berkowitz Elementary School*
> *Chelsea Public Schools, Chelsea, MA*

Pay varies depending on the type of school, with traditional public schools most often having the highest paid teachers. As you review these data, we cannot emphasize enough that these are *averages*, with big swings among districts.

Average Teacher Pay in the United States

Type of School	Average <u>starting</u> salary for a teacher with a college degree	Average salary
Traditional Public	$41,620[a]	$55,600[b]
Charter School (Public)	No data available	$47,000[c]
Private School (Independent)	$30,000[d]	$43,000[e]
Catholic Private High School	$30,410[f]	$39,700[g]

a U.S. Department of Education, National Center for Education Statistics, Schools and Staffing Survey (SASS), "Private School Teacher Data File," 2011-12; and National Teacher and Principal Survey (NTPS), "Public School Teacher Data File," 2015–16. (This table was prepared November 2017.) Retrieved 16 March 2018 from https://nces.ed.gov/programs/digest/d17/tables/dt17_211.10.asp?current=yes) Average is for 2015-16.

b Taie, S., & Goldring, R. (2017, August 17). Characteristics of Public Elementary and Secondary School Teachers in the United States: Results From the 2015–16 National Teacher and Principal Survey. Retrieved 16 March 2018, from https://nces.ed.gov/pubsearch/pubsinfo.asp?pubid=2017072rev. Average is for 2015-16.

c Taie, S., & Goldring, R. (2017, August 17). Characteristics of Public Elementary and Secondary School Teachers in the United States: Results From the 2015–16 National Teacher and Principal Survey. Retrieved 16 March 2018, from https://nces.ed.gov/pubsearch/pubsinfo.asp?pubid=2017072rev. Average is for 2011-12.

d U.S. Department of Education. (This table was prepared May 2013.) Retrieved 26 March 2018 from https://nces.ed.gov/programs/digest/d16/tables/dt16_211.10.asp?current=yes. Average is for 2011-12, all first year.

e Goldring, R., Gray, L., and Bitterman, A. (2013). Characteristics of Public and Private Elementary and Secondary School Teachers in the United States: Results From the 2011–12 Schools and Staffing Survey (NCES 2013-314). U.S. Department of Education. Washington, DC: National Center for Education Statistics. Retrieved 18 March 2018 from https://nces.ed.gov/pubs2013/2013314.pdf. Average is for 2011-12.

f Note that these numbers are only approximate, given that the salaries are for secondary schools; elementary schools' salaries may be up to 20 percent lower. National Association of Catholic School Teachers. (2017). 2016-2017 Lay Teachers' Salaries. Retrieved 26 March 2018 from http://www.nacst.com/salsurvey/2016-2017_SALARY_SURVEY. pdf. Average is for 2016-17.

g U.S. Department of Education. Retrieved 26 March 2018 from https://nces.ed.gov/surveys/sass/tables/sass1112_2013314_t12n_006.asp.

Let's look at starting salaries in a range of districts across the country. Notice the variations not just in the total dollar amounts, but in how far that money can take you when you actually live in that community. Beside the column of salaries for first-year teachers, check out the percentage of that salary required to rent a one-bedroom apartment in that district. A good rule of thumb is that you shouldn't spend more than a third of your paycheck on rent.

Where can a single person afford to live on a starting teacher's salary?[a]

State	School District	2016-2017 Starting Salary	Percent of your paycheck needed to rent a one-bedroom apartment	State	School District	2016-2017 Starting Salary	Percent of your paycheck needed to rent a one-bedroom apartment
Alabama	Mobile	$38,342	19%	Montana	Billings	$37,668	18%
Alaska	Anchorage	$48,886	24%	Nebraska	Omaha	$40,000	20%
Arizona	Mesa	$38,500	23%	Nevada	Clark County	$40,900	21%
Arkansas	Little Rock	$34,865	22%	New Hampshire	Manchester	$37,250	28%
California	Fresno	$45,366	17%	New Jersey	Newark	$51,500	23%
California	Oakland	$44,880	41%	New Mexico	Albuquerque	$34,000	21%
California	San Francisco	$53,672	66%	New York	New York City	$51,650	55%
Colorado	Denver	$40,289	36%	North Carolina	Charlotte-Mecklenburg	$40,247	27%
Connecticut	New Haven	$43,759	27%				
Delaware	Red Clay	$40,543	26%	North Dakota	Bismarck Public	$45,700	17%
District of Columbia	District of Columbia	$51,539	50%	Ohio	Columbus City	$44,043	17%
				Oklahoma	Oklahoma City	$34,000	19%
Florida	Miami-Dade County	$40,800	48%	Oregon	Portland	$38,921	49%
				Pennsylvania	Philadelphia	$41,127	31%
Georgia	Atlanta	$45,600	29%	Rhode Island	Providence	$39,948	28%
Hawaii	Hawaii	$45,963	40%	South Carolina	Greenville County	$34,271	24%
Idaho	West Ada	$37,249	19%	South Dakota	Sioux Falls	$35,752	22%
Illinois	Chicago	$50,653	34%	Tennessee	Metropolitan Nashville	$42,100	35%
Indiana	Indianapolis	$40,000	17%				
Iowa	Des Moines	$40,160	20%	Texas	Austin	$46,810	25%
Kansas	Wichita	$39,146	15%	Texas	Dallas	$50,000	24%
Kentucky	Jefferson County	$42,070	20%	Texas	Houston	$51,500	26%
Louisiana	Jefferson Parish	$40,949	22%	Utah	Granite	$36,714	24%
Maine	Portland	$38,068	37%	Vermont	Burlington	$43,565	25%
Maryland	Baltimore County	$46,053	26%	Virginia	Henrico County	$43,571	25%
Massachusetts	Boston	$52,632	45%	Washington	Seattle	$48,099	34%
Michigan	Detroit	$35,683	19%	West Virginia	Kanawha	$35,094	19%
Minnesota	St. Paul	$44,759	23%	Wisconsin	Milwaukee	$41,311[b]	19%
Mississippi	DeSoto	$37,371	22%	Wyoming	Laramie County	$48,195	15%
Missouri	St. Louis	$39,015	21%				

a   This table uses salary data from NCTQ's Teacher Contract Database (https://www.nctq.org/contract-database/home) and couples it with rental and housing data from Zillow, a real estate website and marketplace that tracks housing and rental prices, as well as the US Census Bureau. For more information, visit https://www.nctq.org/blog/October-2017:-Does-low-pay-shut-teachers-out-of-the-housing-market.

b   Based on new hire salary.

How Do Teachers Earn Raises?

Teachers generally earn three different kinds of raises.

First, there is the annual *cost of living* raise, which is usually quite small, with payouts that will add only several hundred dollars a year to a young teacher's wages.

Second, there are also raises associated with *each year of experience* a teacher accumulates, whereby the teacher would move "up a step" each year on something called a *salary schedule* — which we explain below. Teachers can also earn even more if they earn *graduate credits*. These "step and lane" increases are generally larger than the cost of living raise. Taken together, the annual raise of a public school teacher usually ranges from 1 percent to 5 percent.[35]

The third kind of raise occurs where there is a new labor agreement (often known as the local "teacher contract") or a new state law goes into effect. When this happens, all of the amounts on the salary schedule are revised, and they typically go up. In early 2018, West Virginia teachers gained national attention by walking off the job for nine days to protest low pay and shrinking benefits. The state legislature responded by passing a law providing all teachers with a five percent raise.

Over a thirty-year career, teachers end up earning an average of about $30,000 more per year than when they started, but again, that is an average. There are big differences across school districts. Here are five big districts that appear to have the largest increases in pay, going from the starting salary of a first-year teacher to the maximum salary available in the district — a teacher who probably has a Ph.D and 25 or more years of experience:

- Rochester City School District (NY): increase of $88,439
- Prince William County Public Schools (VA): increase of $68,143
- Pittsburgh Public Schools (PA): increase of $61,691
- Montgomery County Public Schools (MD): increase of $59,837
- New York City Department of Education (NY): increase of $57,161

But here are a few districts where the difference is not nearly so great:

- West Ada School District (ID): increase of $15,965
- Klein Independent School District (TX): increase of $16,400
- Guilford County Schools (NC): increase of $17,670
- Jefferson Parish Public School System (LA): increase of $18,000
- Oklahoma City Public Schools (OK): increase of $19,425[36]

Every district has a document called a salary schedule, which is a chart that tells teachers how much they will earn depending on their total years of experience and credits or degrees earned. The numbers at the far left of this table correspond to the number of years someone has worked in the district. A teacher can move over to a higher base pay by also earning graduate degrees, or at least some credits towards a graduate degree.

Sample Salary Schedule from Boston, MA

	A Bachelor	**B+15** credits	**B** Masters	**M+15** credits	**C** M+30	**M+45** credits	**M+60** credits	**M+75** credits	**D** Doctorate
1	$52,632	$54,449	$56,254	$58,073	$59,886	$61,699	$63,772	$65,571	$66,597
2	$59,103	$61,235	$63,373	$65,514	$67,649	$69,774	$72,175	$74,026	$75,082
3	$62,663	$64,801	$66,935	$69,077	$71,200	$73,345	$75,746	$77,600	$78,656
4	$66,795	$68,373	$70,502	$72,641	$74,773	$76,901	$79,317	$81,167	$82,221
5	$69,795	$72,203	$74,598	$77,002	$79,410	$81,810	$84,475	$86,330	$87,386
6	$73,96	$76,361	$78,766	$81,165	$83,569	$85,965	$88,805	$90,656	$91,712
7	$78,721	$81,120	$83,526	$85,926	$88,331	$90,734	$93,407	$95,260	$96,315
8	$83,532	$85,927	$88,334	$90,734	$93,138	$95,548	$98,215	$100,071	$101,126
9	$87,709	$90,106	$92,510	$94,912	$97,314	$99,726	$102,395	$104,250	$105,304

See if you can read this schedule. Match the description with the salary.[37]

1. A teacher with nine years experience but did not earn an additional graduate credits after a bachelor's degree
2. A starting teacher in Boston who has only a bachelor's degree
3. A teacher who has a master's degree plus an additional 45 credits and nine years of experience
4. A teacher with four years of experience who has earned a master's degree

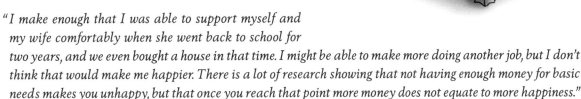

"I make enough that I was able to support myself and my wife comfortably when she went back to school for two years, and we even bought a house in that time. I might be able to make more doing another job, but I don't think that would make me happier. There is a lot of research showing that not having enough money for basic needs makes you unhappy, but that once you reach that point more money does not equate to more happiness."

– Bill Curtin, high school English teacher,
Carbondale Community High School, IL

Beyond Base Pay

So far, we've looked at teachers' base pay, but there are other ways many teachers earn more money. Here are eight such ways, and there are surely others. On average, teachers earn almost $4,000 above their base pay through some of the activities described below.[38] Note that not all districts pay teachers for doing these things.

8 Ways Teachers Increase Their Pay Without Leaving the Classroom

1. Coach a sport or lead an extracurricular club. Teachers who do this during the school year make an average of $2,630 on top of their base salary.[39]

2. Take on a leadership position in the building. Many districts pay extra for positions like "Instructional Coach" or "Mentor Teacher."

3. Earn a bonus for helping students achieve great test results. While only about 6 percent of teachers nationwide earn this merit pay, the average amount they earn is $1,470.[40]

4. Become a National Board Certified Teacher. While bonus amounts vary and are not present in every state, a few states pay $5,000 or more in annual stipends.[41]

5. Work in a really challenging school. Some districts pay a bonus for teachers who teach in a school with high levels of poverty and low overall achievement. The amount teachers can earn for teaching in these schools varies from as little as $100 to as much as $20,000 for highly effective teachers in some schools in the District of Columbia.

6. Teach in a field that has a shortage of teachers. The most common shortage areas are math, science, special education, and English Language Learner Instruction.

7. Change jobs! As most teachers improve in their first three years of teaching, many high-paying districts prefer to hire only experienced teachers.

8. And lastly, much to the regret of many teachers who do not feel they should have to take on additional employment, take a second job during the school year and/or summer employment. *Nearly two-thirds of teachers perform additional work during the school year and about one third take a summer job.*[42] This is especially true for newer teachers. Teachers who work for a school during the summer (often teaching summer school) earn an average of $2,700 on top of their base salary, while teachers who take non-school jobs over the summer earn an average of $4,060.[43]

Benefits

Salaries don't tell the full story. Most professional workers also enjoy a number of benefits and teachers are no exception. What are benefits? They are payments made by your employer on your behalf, such as for health insurance or contributing money towards your retirement — payments that are over and above the salary you will be paid. In addition to paying your salary, an employer generally pays another 33 percent of that salary in benefits. In other words, let's say your starting salary is $45,000. Your district may spend an additional $14,850 to cover a number of benefits, so your real cost to the school district is $59,850 — not $45,000.

Here we show some typical teacher benefits compared to the benefits of people who go into another profession.

Typical Benefits for Public School Teachers

187 work days in a year[a]

13 days off per year on average, but it ranges from as low as 7 to as high as 25[c]

Health insurance:
On average, school districts pay about 84% of the full amount for the employee, but only 65% of the health care cost for the employee's family[e]

Dental:
Districts pay 50% of the cost of dental insurance,[h] with 44% of districts offering some coverage for orthodontics[i]

Vision:
About 34% of teachers work in districts that pay for vision insurance[k]

Retirement:
Nearly all teachers (87%) have access to a retirement plan that offers a guaranteed income after retirement; 77% choose to participate in those kinds of plans. Some teachers (12%) opt out, preferring retirement plans similar to those offered in the private sector.[m]

Typical Benefits for a Professional in the Private Sector

252 work days in a year[b]

22 days off per year on average[d]

Health insurance:
On average, employers pay about 79% of the full amount for the employee[f] but only 67% of the health care cost for the employee's family[g]

Dental:
Employers pay 42% of the cost of dental insurance, with 47% of those plans offering some coverage for orthodontics[j]

Vision:
About 23% of private sector employees have employers who pay for vision insurance[l]

Retirement:
Far fewer private sector employees (62%) have retirement plans that offer a guaranteed income after retirement. Instead, both the employee and the employer contribute a portion of one's salary each year to a retirement account, so the amount an employee will ultimately receive upon retirement cannot be predicted. However, all private sector employees have access to some retirement income from the Social Security system, while many teachers who receive a pension do not.[n]

a. Nittler, K. (2016, August). August 2016: Student and teacher school year. Retrieved 26 October 2018 from https://www.nctq.org/blog/August-2016:-Student-and-teacher-school-year

b. U.S. Bureau of Labor Statistics. (2017, March). National Compensation Survey: Table 33. Paid holidays: Number of days provided, private industry workers,. Retrieved 26 October 2018 from https://www.bls.gov/ncs/ebs/benefits/2017/ownership/private/table33a.pdf

c. Nittler, K., & Alfuth, J. (2016, September). District Trendline: September 2016: Teacher leave. Retrieved 26 October 2018 from https://www.nctq.org/blog/September-2016:-Teacher-leave

d. U.S. Bureau of Labor Statistics. (2017, March). National Compensation Survey: Table 35. Paid sick leave: Number of annual days by service requirement, 1 private industry worker. Retrieved 26 October 2018 from https://www.bls.gov/ncs/ebs/benefits/2017/ownership/private/table35a.pdf and U.S. Bureau of Labor Statistics. (2017, March). National Compensation Survey: Table 38. Paid vacations: Number of annual days by service requirement, 1 private industry workers,. Retrieved 26 October 2018 from https://www.bls.gov/ncs/ebs/benefits/2017/ownership/private/table38a.pdf

e. U.S. Bureau of Labor Statistics. (2017, March). National Compensation Survey: Table 10. Medical care benefits: Share of premiums paid by employer and employee, State and local government workers. Retrieved 26 October 2018 from https://www.bls.gov/ncs/ebs/benefits/2017/ownership/govt/table10a.pdf

f. U.S. Bureau of Labor Statistics. (2017, October 17). The Economics Daily: Vision care plans available to 23 percent of private industry workers in March 2017. Retrieved 26 October 2018 from https://www.bls.gov/opub/ted/2017/vision-care-plans-available-to-23-percent-of-private-industry-workers-in-march-2017.htm

g. U.S. Bureau of Labor Statistics. (2017, March). National Compensation Survey: Table 10. Medical care benefits: Share of premiums paid by employer and employee, private industry workers,. Retrieved 26 October 2018 from https://www.bls.gov/ncs/ebs/benefits/2017/ownership/private/table10a.pdf

h. U.S. Bureau of Labor Statistics. (2007, September). National Compensation Survey: Employee Benefits in State and Local Governments in the United States. Retrieved 26 October 2018 from https://www.bls.gov/ncs/ebs/sp/ebsm0007.pdf

i. U.S. Bureau of Labor Statistics. (2011). National Compensation Survey: Table 46. Dental care benefits: Coverage for orthodontia, state and local government workers, National Compensation Survey. Retrieved 26 October 2018 from https://www.bls.gov/ncs/ebs/detailedprovisions/2011/ownership/govt/table46a.pdf

j. U.S. Bureau of Labor Statistics. (2015). Table 38. Dental care benefits: Coverage for orthodontia, private industry workers. Retrieved 26 October 2018 from https://www.bls.gov/ncs/ebs/detailedprovisions/2015/ownership/private/table38a.pdf

k. U.S. Bureau of Labor Statistics. (2007, September). National Compensation Survey: Employee Benefits in State and Local Governments in the United States. Retrieved 26 October 2018 from https://www.bls.gov/ncs/ebs/sp/ebsm0007.pdf

l. U.S. Bureau of Labor Statistics. (2017, October 13). The Economics Daily: Vision care plans available to 23 percent of private industry workers in March 2017. Retrieved 26 October 2018 from https://www.bls.gov/opub/ted/2017/vision-care-plans-available-to-23-percent-of-private-industry-workers-in-march-2017.htm

m. U.S. Bureau of Labor Statistics. (2016, September). National Compensation Survey: Employee Benefits in the United States, March 2016. Retrieved 26 October 2018 from https://www.bls.gov/ncs/ebs/benefits/2016/ebbl0059.pdf

n. U.S. Bureau of Labor Statistics. (2017, March). National Compensation Survey: Table 2. Retirement benefits: Access, participation, and take-up rates, 1 private industry workers,. Retrieved 26 October 2018 from https://www.bls.gov/ncs/ebs/benefits/2017/ownership/private/table02a.pdf

A Day in the Life of a High School English Teacher
By Bill Curtin

My school day starts in the office, where I grab coffee and check my mailbox. There's nothing but junk — because anything important is emailed — but the ritual feels nice.

Mornings are easier now that I don't have to create everything from scratch. I just tweak things here and there, remembering last year's stumbling blocks. Satisfied, I print today's handouts, take them to the copier, and grade a few papers while I wait.

When the bell rings, I turn on some music and greet students at the door. I've asked the Creative Writing class to define poetry, and while they write I take attendance, hand back papers, and give Rose an assignment she missed yesterday. Then I welcome everyone and ask them to create a common definition in small groups. I wander around, listening in and responding to questions:

"Mr. Curtin, do poems have to rhyme?"

"Have you ever read poems that didn't?"

After a few minutes, I get their attention again: "Based on your definitions, tell me if what I write is a poem. OK?"

Heads nod.

I turn to the board and write a single word: *lighght*. "Is this a poem?"

Heads shake. Furiously.

"Well, it won a national award, so maybe your definitions need work."

Angry objections start flying. I smile. Success. I know they're hooked, and this class will be fun, as I question their assumptions and prod them to think deeply.

Sixth hour is different: mandatory sophomore English.

We start with a quiz, and I know right away that most didn't read, because I've already been asked four times if retakes were allowed. I begin reading aloud, pausing to ask questions, selecting students randomly: "Austin?"

"Um, cuz she's poor?"

"Yes. Why does that make her speak differently?"

"I dunno."

I stare him down.

"...is it, because...her parents, like, didn't teach her, cuz they didn't know?"

"Jemyra, what do you think about what Austin said?"

"Um, yeah. Cuz she's poor."

It's like pulling teeth. A hand shoots up — a *volunteer*! Finally, a critical thought! "Yes, Cameron?"

"Can I go to the bathroom?"

The bell puts sixth hour out of its misery, and I shout a homework reminder as they leave. Tomorrow's reading quiz will be no better, but I know they'll be hooked by chapter six.

As the room empties, I shuffle the day's papers into stacks. I have ten minutes before Creative Writing Club meets. They walk in and eagerly tackle today's prompt. An hour later they leave, excited about our student anthology project.

After they're gone, I call three parents to say their students didn't read. I can't call them all, but eventually word will get around that I take it seriously. I thumb my stack of papers and decide they can wait until tomorrow — it's almost 5:00.

On the way out, the janitor jokes about leaving "early" today — we're often the last ones there. But tonight I'm working from home, leading a webinar for teachers working on National Board Certification. That leaves just enough time for dinner with my wife and a movie before bed. Of course, I'll only be half watching — I'll be busy remembering things I need to do tomorrow, and that stack of grading that got bigger today.

Bill Curtin has taught high school English in Carbondale, IL for 11 years.

Chapter 5:
You Are in the Driver's Seat

Your early success as a teacher will be influenced by decisions you make now, before you even begin college. The college you select and the specific courses you choose to take will matter a lot in your development. This chapter shows you how to customize your college experience to meet your needs, so that you will be more likely to be fully ready to teach when you graduate.

Preparing to Teach in Three Parts

To be "classroom-ready" upon graduation, you will need to build knowledge and skills in three areas: *subject knowledge*, *professional knowledge*, and *practice*. Think of these areas as a puzzle in which you put all the right pieces together. If there's a piece missing, you won't be fully prepared. That doesn't mean you can't go on to eventually become a successful teacher. It just means your journey will be much harder, as much of your learning will have to be on the job. We call that kind of start to teaching a "trial by fire."

One of the hard truths we have to deliver to you in this chapter is that the top programs featured in the back of this book are not typical. Most preparation programs fall short in providing their students with the knowledge, skills, and practice that you will need. In one survey of education school alumni, 62 percent of the respondents said that their program did not prepare them to cope with classroom reality.[44] That's why we want to help you pick the best program for you, as well as provide you with guidance to fill gaps not addressed by your program. That way, even if you ultimately do attend a program that is not excellent at preparing teachers, you will be able to shore up some of the program's weaknesses.

Let's dig in.

The Subject Knowledge Teachers Need

The specific skills and knowledge a teacher needs certainly depend on the grade and subjects she'll be teaching. No one expects a high school biology teacher to be ready to teach about phonics and conversely, no one expects a first-grade teacher to understand the best methods for teaching trigonometry.

Teaching elementary grades: The subject knowledge you need

We know a lot about what the 1.5 million elementary teachers teaching in the U.S. need to know. However, some colleges don't cover all of the necessary bases, leaving many new elementary teachers with topics or subjects they are not ready to teach. That's why we provide detailed guidance here.

It's especially important to know which courses to take because it may mean the difference between qualifying for a teaching license or not. To receive a teaching license, almost every state requires its teacher candidates to pass a test of the four subjects that are taught in elementary grades: English language arts, science, social studies, and mathematics (see page 27). What you may not know is that more than half of all teacher candidates fail these tests at least once. These tests cost a lot of money to take over and over again — for a commonly required four-part exam, taking the full exam costs $170, and retaking any one section costs $60 each time. More importantly, you generally won't be in a position at that point to take the courses you need to do better, as most programs won't require you to take the test until you're close to graduation

It's not just these licensing tests that are such a stumbling block to getting a job. They serve as a critical signal that when you eventually do get a teaching job, you may face difficulty teaching the typical content found in the elementary curriculum. Nearly two thirds of all teachers responded to a 2011 government survey stating that they did not feel very well prepared to teach — and those are the teachers who presumably passed their tests![45]

The bottom line is even if you think you have a handle on the content, you might not. Let's be safe, not sorry. No matter how great a student someone may be, there are knowledge gaps that need filling. Your responsibility when you get to college will be to manage your gaps.

Here are the 15 broad topics that every elementary teacher should know something about, not only because these topics are found on many of the state licensing tests, but because they will make you a more effective and interesting teacher:

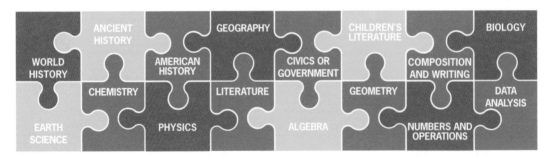

You may find this a bit puzzling (haha!) and possibly overwhelming. Remember that you are not starting from scratch. You probably learned a lot about these topics in your high school courses. That's especially true if you took any AP courses or high-quality survey courses.

Most colleges require you to spend a couple of years fulfilling your "general graduation requirements" before you start taking courses in your major. Typically, you will have to take anywhere from 10 to 18 courses, depending on the college. The choices they will give you may not necessarily be relevant to what you need to know as an elementary teacher, so if you aren't planning ahead, you may find yourself unready to take the state licensing test. You can do yourself a big favor by choosing only those general education courses that align with what you need to know to pass your state's elementary content test, as well as the curriculum you will one day be asked to teach.

Here are some tips for choosing the right "general education" courses:

Tip #1. As an elementary teacher, you don't need to become an expert but you do need to know the fundamental concepts in each of the 15 areas.

If you can't remember the details of the War of 1812 or Prohibition, it's okay. However, if you don't know what Prohibition was or you can't remember when and why these wars happened — the Civil War, World War II, or the American Revolution — you will want to take a course in American history that covers a big span of American history, not a course that only focuses on a single decade or issue.

Examples of ideal courses if you are weak in American history:

- American History to 1865 (Pre-Columbian times to the Civil War)
- Introduction to Modern American History, a survey of the major political, social, cultural, diplomatic, and economic developments since 1865
- Introduction to American Politics, covering basic principles of the government of the United States

Your college may offer some hyper-specific history courses about individual eras or themes. These are less important to your teacher preparation than the broad survey courses. If your overall American history knowledge is weak, we recommend avoiding them. Here are some examples of the kinds of courses to avoid if you still need to strengthen your general historical knowledge:

- Sex and Western Society, teaching perspectives on sexual practices, ideologies, and identities in the Western World
- America in the Sixties, the major political, social, cultural, diplomatic, and economic developments of the period
- American government and politics through the lens of religion

The same rules apply to all subjects for college courses, not just history. A course on volcanoes might seem great, as you're likely to teach about volcanoes, but it's not the only geology you'll need to know. If you are weak in geology, take a broader introductory geology course. You'll need the broader foundational knowledge if you are going to fill an entire year of science lessons for your fourth graders.

Tip #2. Choose courses covering content where you know your knowledge is weak, not where you are already strong!

We know it is tempting to take a class that you already aced in high school. Still we encourage you to take that basic chemistry class if you previously struggled to pass it. You don't want to be reading about the periodic table the night before you have to teach it. Also, the licensing tests you need to take will definitely ask you some basic chemistry questions, so you need to get prepared!

Here are examples of ideal courses if you have fundamental knowledge gaps in elementary science topics (earth science, chemistry, physics, or biology):

- Biology I: Cells to Organisms, biological concepts from cells to structure/functions of organisms
- General Chemistry I: the basic concepts of chemistry
- Elementary Physics I: an introduction to Newtonian mechanics
- Physical Science: understanding the non-living world through astronomy, chemistry, physics, and geology

Tip #3: Choose courses that are most likely to benefit your future students.

If a college gives you a choice of several different courses, be sure to think about which ones will be most relevant for the range of topics you'll be teaching your students in a few years. If you dig enough into the district or school websites where you think you want to land a teaching job, you can typically find information on what is taught there. Use that knowledge to plan for what courses to take. Once again, very specific courses focused on a single topic probably won't take you very far in building your subject knowledge to be an effective elementary teacher.

Avoid courses like these:

- Physics of Movies, in which students watch and analyze short movie clips that demonstrate interesting, unusual, or impossible physics.
- The Social History of Popular Music in 20th-Century America, exploring the relationship between popular music and major developments in 20th-century America.
- Sport and American History, surveying American sport history, from the colonial era to the present.
- History of Dance in Western Civilization, exploring dance in its creative and historical aspects.
- Topics in Foreign Film, a literature course examining topics in film including the film traditions of other nations.

NCTQ has a valuable online tool, Path to Teach, to help you understand which courses to take. We've looked at the course requirements at about 1,200 elementary programs and can tell you where they come up short, so you know where you need to concentrate your efforts. To look up the colleges you are considering attending, go to www.pathtoteach.org.

Teaching middle or high school grades: The subject knowledge you need

Now let's look at the subject area requirements for teaching secondary levels, that is, middle or high school. The major difference between the preparation of secondary and elementary teachers is the need for secondary teachers to become experts in the subject(s) they want to teach.

Becoming an English or mathematics teacher is relatively straightforward. You will major in English or math, which typically means taking around 15 courses in your subject, as well as completing some kind of larger capstone project. However, the preparation someone needs to teach either social studies or science can be much more complicated, as many colleges don't offer a "social studies" or "general science" major.

Let's go over why these two subjects pose such problems and how you can avoid getting stuck having to teach a subject you barely know.

What kinds of secondary licenses are in my state?

State	Mathematics	English	Biology	Chemistry	Physics	Earth Science	Physical Science	General Science	History	Political Science	Economics	Geography	Psychology	Sociology	Anthropology	Social Studies
Alabama																
Alaska																
Arizona																
Arkansas																
California																
Colorado																
Connecticut																
Delaware																
District of Columbia																
Florida																
Georgia																
Hawaii																
Idaho																
Illinois			†	†	†	†			†	†	†	†	†	†	†	
Indiana																
Iowa																
Kansas																
Kentucky																
Louisiana																
Maine																
Maryland																
Massachusetts									†	†						
Michigan																
Minnesota																
Mississippi																
Missouri																
Montana																
Nebraska																
Nevada			†													
New Hampshire																
New Jersey																
New Mexico																
New York																
North Carolina																
North Dakota																
Ohio																
Oklahoma									†	†	†	†	†	†		
Oregon			†	†	†											
Pennsylvania																
Rhode Island																
South Carolina																
South Dakota																
Tennessee																
Texas																
Utah																
Vermont																
Virginia																
Washington										†						
West Virginia																
Wisconsin																
Wyoming																

Legend:

■ Required certification tests ensure that you know the subjects you will teach

■ Required certification tests do not ensure that you know all the subjects you will teach OR no tests are required

□ Certification not offered

† This single subject certification permits you to teach multiple subjects. For example, you could be certified in biology but teach physics.

Some states limit science teachers to teaching only one subject (e.g. chemistry), which, like English or math, simply requires a chemistry major. However, other states offer general science certification that permits a teacher to teach all of the sciences: biology, chemistry, earth science, physics, and more.

The range of topics a teacher can cover is even broader for social studies. Almost the entire country (forty-seven states and the District of Columbia) allows teachers to earn a license in *"general social studies,"* which permits teachers to teach courses in history, government, geography, and economics, as well as the behavioral sciences, like psychology and sociology.

Choosing a secondary license

Let's take a closer look at secondary teacher licenses. At this level, unlike elementary teaching, the licenses tend to describe the subject you'll be teaching such as "English Language Arts," rather than the grade levels.

Take a look below at the handy chart of all the different types of licenses every state allows. If you want to teach biology in Texas, for example, you could earn either a *life science* license or a *general science* license. There are benefits and drawbacks to both. If you pursue the life science license, you will probably be very well prepared to teach biology, the only subject you can teach. If you pursue the general science certification, you will find it easier to get a job because you can teach more subjects — that is, if you are willing to teach more subjects. Given the persistent shortages of science teachers in most communities, it is fairly easy to find science teaching jobs even if you have opted to specialize in only one subject. For example, essentially every district is looking for a good physics teacher.

If you want to teach history in Colorado, the state's social science certification is your only option. If you live in Maryland, you could choose between the single-subject history certification or the multiple-subject *social studies* certification.

Of course, if you want to be a math or English teacher, your answer will be simple, because states take the same approach to licenses in these two subject areas. Completing a mathematics or English major in college will serve as part of your teaching license requirements.

If you seek a general certification for science or social studies, it will be largely up to you to make sure your coursework covers all the bases of what you may be asked to teach. Do not count on your college automatically knowing what this may be. Also, as the chart below shows, the state tests don't always tell you either. For instance, while taking 30 credits of biology will give you an excellent understanding of human anatomy, cell structures, and biochemistry, you will be pretty unhappy if your principal requires you to then teach a physics course because you have a general science certification. For science teachers in particular, plan carefully for what you may be eventually asked to teach.

On top of the subject requirements, all teachers need to learn how to teach their intended subject. It's one thing to know how to solve for x; it's another thing to know how to teach it so your students aren't confused, and then to anticipate and help them through a wide range of potential misunderstandings. A course that shows you how to teach is called a "methods course," which is why it is a problem when a teacher prep program only offers a general methods course, grouping all secondary candidates together to learn teaching methods across all subjects, with little time spent on the specific challenges associated with teaching students algebra, how to write a good paragraph, or conducting a science experiment for 25 students at a time. As a secondary teacher, you absolutely need to learn teaching methods that are specific to your subject area.

Charting your preparation to teach at the middle or high school levels

Subject	Things to Consider
English	You should get the equivalent of a major in English.
	Remember, though, that you'll be teaching non-fiction, literature, and poetry — so take courses that will overlap with the typical high school curriculum. Familiarize yourself with key authors in literature, such as Homer, Shakespeare, Steinbeck, Morrison, and so on.
	This appendix (http://www.corestandards.org/assets/Appendix_B.pdf) has a set of examples to get you started.
	Also, you'll be teaching writing, speaking, and research skills, so look for courses to strengthen your expertise in those areas, too.
	Take a methods course to help you teach your students how to analyze texts, write, and research, as well as helping you design assessments so you know what they've learned and what they still need to learn.
Mathematics	You should get the equivalent of a major in mathematics.
	Remember, you likely won't teach advanced topics like topology or real analysis in high school, so while you should take some upper-level mathematics in college, make certain your algebra, geometry, trigonometry, calculus, probability, and statistics expertise is solid.
	Also, consider some computer science coursework.
	You should take a methods course to help you learn how to teach mathematics, to anticipate common errors students make, and to design assessments (assignments, quizzes, tests, etc.) in the subject.
Science	While we recommend a major in the sciences based on what you want to teach — if it's high school biology, then major in biology — you need to prepare yourself carefully depending on the secondary certifications in your state.
	Refer back to the secondary certifications chart. Are you thinking about general science for your state? If so, you'll need to make certain that you take as much science as possible to strengthen your expertise across all of the sciences you could potentially be assigned to teach.
	A reasonable distribution of courses to prepare to teach science at the middle or high school levels might look as follows:

Subject	3-credit courses
Biology	**4**
Focus on courses that teach you biological structure and function (for example, how the structure of DNA determines protein shape); matter and energy in organisms and ecosystems (for example, how photosynthesis works); interdependencies in ecosystems (the food chain, population cycles); inheritance, natural selection, and evolution.	
Chemistry/Physics	**7**
Take courses that teach you about the structure and properties of matter (such as the periodic table); chemical reactions (for example, how they can be explained by the outermost electron states of atoms and the periodic table); forces and interactions (such as Newton's second law of motion and Law of Gravitation); energy (like kinetic and thermal); waves and electromagnetic radiation (light and radio, for example).	
Earth Science	**2**
Look for courses that teach you about space, the history of the Earth and its systems, and weather and climate.	

Social Studies Most states offer a certification allowing teachers to teach multiple subjects falling under the broad term "social studies."

You should take a decent set of U.S. and world history courses, as this is most of what social studies teachers teach in middle and high school. Round out your 15-course major with 2 to 4 political science courses, a geography course, 2 economics courses, and some electives in the social sciences (like anthropology and sociology) to cover as many bases as you can.

A reasonable distribution of courses to prepare to teach middle or high school social studies might look as follows:

Subject	3-credit courses
History	8

Focus on broad survey courses of early and modern U.S. history (from colonization and revolution through the Civil War and to the modern era) and ancient and modern world history (from prehistoric times through the first river valley civilizations; the development of kingdoms and societies in Africa, Asia, the Middle East, Europe, and the Americas; the Renaissance; exploration and colonization; industrial revolution; World Wars; through modern times). Your state may also require a state history course (e.g. Texas history).

Political Science/Government	4

Take courses that study the U.S. Constitution, governmental institutions and policy-making practice, and citizen participation principles that form the basis of U.S. government and politics. Consider also courses that compare governments and practices across countries.

Economics	2

Look for courses offering a broad introduction to microeconomics (focusing on the actions and choices of individuals) and macroeconomics (focusing on large-scale — national or international — choices and processes).

Geography	1

Enroll in a survey course that studies the history and patterns of human interaction with the natural environment.

Psychology	1

Focus on a course that introduces you to the scientific study of human behavior and thinking, including topics like the biological bases of behavior, perception, learning, and motivation.

Sociology or Anthropology	1

Find an introduction to sociology or anthropology course.

Advanced Placement (AP) History and Social Sciences course guides are a great reference: https://apcentral.collegeboard.org/courses

You should take a methods course to help you learn how to teach history or one of these other subjects so that you can build deep understandings of important concepts, anticipate common errors that students make, and design assessments in the subject.

Professional Knowledge

Now let's talk about the next big puzzle piece, Professional Knowledge — what you need to know about the practice of teaching and how children learn. Here's a quick list of just some of the things that fall under professional knowledge:

1. Reflecting on teaching experiences and making thoughtful adjustments accordingly.

2. Designing tests and assessments in the subject you are teaching.

3. Anticipating and correcting common mistakes students will make.

4. Becoming "culturally competent" by respecting all community members' cultures and including them respectfully in the classroom.

5. Recognizing and correcting when you are not treating all students with fairness and equity.

6. Interpreting the results of standardized tests and planning strategic next steps based on those interpretations.

7. Communicating constructively with parents and guardians.

8. Adjusting instruction for children who do not speak English.

9. Gaining a working knowledge of state laws and regulations every teacher needs to know, particularly regarding discipline, special education, and student learning standards.

10. Knowing how to anticipate and to manage a range of student behaviors, from common misbehavior like talking out of turn to more serious incidents like a student destroying classroom materials.

11. Understanding core strategies that are most likely to boost student learning, such as questioning techniques.

12. Learning and implementing core strategies that will help students retain what they learn.

13. Monitoring and measuring student progress.

14. Utilizing different approaches to teaching the same material, depending upon what works.

15. Composing engaging, coherent unit- and lesson-plans.

16. Using technology to help manage your classes (grading, attendance) and, even more importantly, teaching your subjects (lab equipment, simulation software, etc.).

17. And lastly, but most importantly for elementary teachers: knowing how to teach children to read, including knowing what to do with students of any age who are struggling with reading. There is a real science to teaching reading and you need to learn it.

Some of this content will be covered by your program, but unfortunately we can tell you that a lot of this content is often missing. Also, some content in college courses about teaching is not grounded in research despite a vast body of scientific knowledge about effective teaching practices. NCTQ can provide some of this information, including how programs approach managing student misbehavior and learning how to teach reading — two of the most essential on this list.

The sad reality is that a huge number of novice teachers end up scrambling to fill in many of these gaps after they've started to teach, catching veteran teachers in the hall for some quick advice or conducting late-night internet searches. We've seen ten-year veteran teachers break down into tears, learning for the first time how they could have been much more successful from the start if their preparation had exposed them to some of these essential, research-backed approaches.

What can you do to fill other gaps in the essential professional knowledge that every teacher needs?

Here are a few tips:

- If you are attending a large university with many professors teaching the same required Education Psychology or reading course, do some investigating on which professors do the best job.

- Many teachers report that their student teaching experience is a life saver (more on that below) that fills in many gaps they otherwise would have had.

- Keep in mind everything you need to know about teaching does exist out there; you don't need to reinvent the wheel. The most trustworthy source is the Institute for Education Sciences, an agency within the federal government, which has published 19 "What Works Clearinghouse" guides (https://ies.ed.gov/ncee/wwc/PracticeGuides) aimed just at teachers, giving them the knowledge they need to become more effective.

Practice

The information that you will learn in your college courses is important, but you also need a chance to practice what you learn about teaching in real classroom settings. For example, only hands-on experience in a real classroom will help you get a feel for maintaining the right pace, tailoring the activities to your individual students, and including all that you need to cover in the 45 minutes before lunch.

Typical teacher preparation programs include a number of these experiences, but student teaching is the longest, most intense, and most important. It also typically comes last. During student teaching, you'll spend a semester or more in the classroom of a mentor teacher (sometimes called "cooperating teacher") who, ideally, has been chosen because he or she has the skills, dispositions, and experience to be a quality mentor.

Many teachers say that student teaching was the most important part of their training.[46] But despite its importance, we have learned that many teacher preparation programs usually leave far too much about the experience to chance, including the quality of the mentor teacher.

Here are some of the most important features of a high-quality clinical program:

1. When preparing to teach, your student teaching experience should *not* be your first time in a real classroom. Your program should provide you with a number of observation experiences early in your preparation — even in your first year.

2. Your student teaching experience should start when children start their school year, not necessarily when you start college classes. If you miss the start of school because you're still working a summer job, you will have missed the most important tone-setting period in the school year.

3. Your student teaching assignment should be in approximately the same grade and subject you plan on teaching. You shouldn't be assigned to a kindergarten class if you plan on teaching 4th or 5th grade.

4. Representatives from your program should frequently visit you (at least 4 times in a semester) and observe you teaching, providing both written and oral feedback each time.

5. Your mentor teacher should be a great teacher because you need to learn what to do from someone who knows how too do it.

6. You should be provided with opportunities to learn how to handle a wide variety of learning situations, such as being able to work with small or large groups, how to introduce new topics, how to structure whole-class discussions, etc.

7. You should be asked to practice and in return receive expert advice on how to manage a range of student misbehavior.

8. Your clinical experiences should give you exposure to all students from all kinds of backgrounds and abilities. These experiences should be focused on showing you how to be successful with all kinds of kids — not just teaching you how difficult it can be to teach kids who may not look like you.

In this book, we tell you about the programs that are doing a good job providing candidates with a high quality student teaching experience. We recognize that there aren't enough of them out there. However, you may well get lucky, no matter how your program is set up, and be assigned a great mentor teacher. The bottom line is that as long as you remain aware of the pitfalls and are willing to be a relentless, proactive advocate for your preparation, we're confident you will come out ahead.

Chapter 6:
Top Teacher Prep Programs

For nearly 20 years, the National Council on Teacher Quality has been working to help future teachers identify the right teacher preparation program by reviewing more than 2,600 programs in 1,100 colleges across the country. It's why we've written this book to highlight 117 of the best undergraduate teacher preparation programs in 38 states.

Great programs come in all sizes and shapes. Some are private and some are public. Some cost a lot, while others are bargains. Some are located in cities and some are in suburban or rural areas. Some are huge programs, graduating over 1,000 new teachers a year, while some are relatively small.

Some programs excel at preparing secondary teachers, while others have terrific results preparing elementary teachers. There are some that do both quite well. You will find all of them listed in this book.

As you browse these pages, you may notice a few states missing, notably California. That's because prior to 2018, California required all teacher prep programs to provide training at the graduate school level to people who had already earned a bachelor's degree in another subject. Almost all of its programs are at the graduate level. The other states missing from our list — Connecticut, District of Columbia, Hawaii, Kentucky, Maine, Nevada, New Hampshire, New Mexico, Oregon, Rhode Island, Vermont, and Washington — do not have programs that earned our high quality designation. But we're confident they are working on that problem, so stay tuned!

NCTQ bases our evaluation of programs on a set of fundamental indicators of quality.

Here's what we look for, why we look for it, and the information that we gather to be able to reach a judgment.

Rigorous Admissions Process

Various components used in program admissions requirements are examined, such as GPA, scores on aptitude exams, and auditions to determine if the academic aptitude of aspiring teachers is adequately considered among other important criteria.

Learning How to Teach Reading (*elementary only*)

Reading courses and textbooks are combed for evidence that they align with the science learned from five decades of research to equip you with the strategies you need to make sure all of your students can read when they leave your classroom.

Preparing to Teach Math (*elementary only*)

Mathematics courses and texts are examined by experts to determine if teacher candidates will gain the deep conceptual knowledge of the math content topics commonly taught in K-6 mathematics.

Content Preparation – Sciences (*secondary only*)

Course requirements and state licensure tests are examined to determine if aspiring science teachers are likely to possess adequate content knowledge in each of the science subjects they will be certified to teach. An additional review is completed to determine if a course specifically focuses on how to teach the sciences is required.

Content Preparation – Social Studies (*secondary only*)

NCTQ experts review course requirements and licensure tests for potential social studies teachers in the context of the state certifications. Like science, some states certify social studies teachers in a single subject (like history) while others certify teachers in multiple subjects (like history, economics, government, and sociology). Because aspiring teachers must know the subjects they will teach, our evaluation looks for deep content knowledge in the license subject in the former case and across multiple subjects in the latter case. Additionally, course requirements are examined to determine if a course specifically focuses on how to teach the social studies is required.

Learning to Manage the Classroom

We look to see that programs guide faculty observers to provide feedback to student teachers on classroom management strategies supported by research.

High Quality Practice Teaching

A wide variety of documentation is collected from both the program and the school districts where student teachers are placed, including student teaching handbooks, course syllabi, observation forms, and other communications. We look at the qualifications of your mentor teacher and how often faculty visit you while you're student teaching to give you advice on your instruction.

Outstanding Programs

While all of the programs in this list are great, we indicate which are in the top 5 percent with this symbol: .

Institutional Characteristics

We also used 2017 data collected by the U.S. Department of Education for College Scorecard, their online clearinghouse of school information, located at https://collegescorecard.ed.gov/. It has data such as size (large is more than 15,000 students and small is less than 2,000 students), the proportion of students who graduate within six years, whether education is one of top five largest programs at the school, and the average debt students have upon graduating. Typical starting salaries for new teachers in each state are from the 2013 data from National Education Association.[47]

Finally, we talked to deans, students, and alumni at some programs to get highlights and an insider perspective.

Now, turn the page to start your journey!

Appalachian State University
Boone, NC

SCORE CARD
Secondary Indicators of Quality
Rigorous admissions process: **A**

Content preparation (social studies, science): **A**

High quality practice teaching: **C**

Learning to manage the classroom: **C**

62% GRADUATE AND GO RIGHT INTO TEACHING

What's special
Dean's Statement

Preparing quality educators is a cornerstone of Appalachian State University's past, present and future. The state and region look first to Appalachian for innovative instruction, faculty excellence, and student success and engagement. Because we are committed to providing the most authentic experiences possible, a faculty/director from the College of Arts and Sciences supports all disciplinary programs in secondary education. This is a major commitment that facilitates communication and expands opportunities and support systems for students. Secondary education students are provided with a unique perspective – a rich content background provided in the discipline coupled with the expertise of education faculty in the pedagogy of effective instruction. Students enrolled in undergraduate secondary teacher education programs have the opportunity to gain early and sustained success through a blend of clinical and classroom experiences in programs based on content knowledge, creativity, innovation, and collaboration. These authentic learning experiences are essential to the preparation of secondary teacher education students and ensure that our candidates are well prepared to share expertise in their discipline, sustain education within their communities, and inspire the next generation of teachers.

Dr. Melba Spooner, Dean
Reich College of Education, Appalachian State University

Where do candidates student teach?
- Watauga County Schools
- Ashe County Schools
- Wake County Schools

Where do graduates work?
- Charlotte-Mecklenburg School District
- Wake County Schools
- Winston-Salem Forsyth County Schools

Campus Facts at a Glance
Size: Large

Location: Town

Acceptance rate: 68%

Student to faculty ratio: 16 to 1

6-year graduation rate: 70%

Is education a top 5 major: No

Financial
In-state tuition: $7,136

Out-of-state tuition: $21,652

Students receiving federal loans: 47%

Typical debt: $20,500

Typical North Carolina new teacher salary: **$30,778**

What's special about Appalachian State University

Candidates' Observations

The Secondary Education Program at Appalachian State University is unique in that it focuses on strengthening all aspects and characteristics of prospective teachers. This program not only equips future educators with the knowledge necessary to become masters of their chosen subjects but also ensures they possess the traits and characteristics that great teachers embody. Appalachian State's Secondary Education Program prepares students to make the transition from good students to prominent and inspiring teachers.

I recommend Appalachian State University's Secondary Education Program because of the unique opportunities that the program offers to prospective teachers. Students are given the opportunity to enter the classroom early in their education, allowing for real world observation, student connections, and learning. Students in this program receive an ample amount of real world experience and interactions that allow them to grow and learn through hands-on experience, which really makes all the difference.

Chris Tarnowski
English Education Major

I would recommend Appalachian's Secondary Education program because of how early they get you into schools to get real hands-on experience. I was in internships in classrooms starting my first year, and this really helped me start developing skills I could use in the classroom early on while also helping me know for sure that education was the field I wanted to enter.

Even though being a secondary education major means you're split between two colleges within the university, Appalachian has always done an amazing job of making both feel like home. From clubs like Appalachian Educators to the camaraderie that develops in the free use labs the geology department has, I've always felt like I truly belonged in both colleges, something that I feel is pretty rare.

Anthony Wade
Geology, Secondary Education Major

I cannot recommend Appalachian State's secondary education program enough. As a future high school English teacher, it is important to me that I am receiving instruction not only on the content that I will one day be teaching but on methods for how to teach it effectively. I feel confident in my knowledge of literature, language, and media literacy, and I look forward to one day sharing that knowledge in a classroom of my own.

I have also been encouraged every step of the way to think critically and productively about curriculum, assessment, and equity in education; courses dedicated to unpacking and rethinking these subjects have been some of my favorites. I am also thankful to have had professors and mentors in the Reich College of Education who model the kind of empathy and expertise that I hope to one day embody for my students.

My time at App State has empowered me with the skills and the confidence necessary to turn my passion for education into action. I cannot wait to use all that I have learned in the "real world" very soon, but I also do not want to leave!

Kelly Dancy
English Education Major

Bethel University
Saint Paul, MN

Outstanding
Program

SCORE CARD
Elementary Indicators of Quality

Rigorous admissions process:	**A+**
Learning how to teach reading:	**A**
Preparing to teach math:	**A**
High quality practice teaching:	**C**
Learning to manage the classroom:	**B**

96% (2014–2015) **95%** (2015–2016)
GRADUATE AND GO RIGHT INTO TEACHING

What's special

Dean's Statement

New students considering Bethel's award-winning education program would be interested to know that as an institution, an important part of our mission is to educate and energize men and women for excellence in leadership, scholarship, and service. This comes to life in the education department as we prepare future educators. We go beyond books and theories to provide significant, hands-on learning opportunities in a number of diverse settings, including working with evolving education technology. Meaningful and life-changing student learning experiences range from immersive local engagement through the Frogtown/Summit University Community Partnership in Saint Paul, Minnesota to semesters abroad—each adding to the depth of knowledge and experience in preparation of becoming an exceptional teacher. An education degree from Bethel is a game changer. Our unique Block I and Block II models expose students to increasing amounts of real-world experience that directly builds upon the work they do in the classroom. Educators in the field comment that Bethel students come to placements prepared and motivated by purpose and mission. University wide, nearly 9 out 10 of seniors surveyed say they'd come here all over again.

Deborah L. Sullivan-Trainor, Ph.D.
Vice President and Dean, College of Arts & Sciences, Bethel University

Where do candidates student teach?
- Anoka-Hennepin School District
- Fridley School District
- Mounds View School District

Where do graduates work?
- Anoka-Hennepin School District
- White Bear Lake School District
- Hmong College Prep Academy

Campus Facts at a Glance

Size:	Medium
Location:	Suburban
Acceptance rate:	82%
Student to faculty ratio:	11 to 1
Graduation rate:	74%
Is education a top 5 major:	Yes

Financial

Tuition:	$35,160
In-state average annual cost:	$26,602
Students receiving federal loans:	66%
Typical debt:	$24,400
Typical Minnesota new teacher salary:	**$34,505**

What's special about Bethel University

Candidates' Observations

The Education Department at Bethel University focuses on developing the best educators for the field. Throughout my time at Bethel I knew that the department was supporting my future career through the courses, professors, and atmosphere.

Audrey Erdahl '16

Bethel's education program has prepared me to be a successful educator. I provide my students with engaging, effective, and differentiated instruction. Bethel has instilled me with a love for learning and I try to do the same for my students.

Paige Davis '16
First Grade Spanish Immersion Teacher
at Princeton Primary School

I believe the education I received at Bethel prepared me for my role as a teacher, leader, and for my current role as principal. The education department's theme of servant leadership provided a framework and vision for me in all I do, regardless of my position. It helped create the understanding that education is not about me but about the students and families we serve.

Nathan Flansburg '97
Principal, Valentine Hills Elementary, Arden Hills, Minnesota

---

I would recommend this program because the education department is constantly willing to answer questions and work with students to achieve success. The professors are very willing to help and are passionate about the subject of education.

Bethel equipped me to be a strong educator in my field of study. This program offered more hands-on experiences than other programs, which is why I initially chose Bethel, besides the faith-based campus and its high rank in education.

Cedarville University
Cedarville, OH

SCORE CARD
Elementary Indicators of Quality

Rigorous admissions process:	A
Learning how to teach reading:	D
Preparing to teach math:	A+
High quality practice teaching:	C
Learning to manage the classroom:	**Not reviewed**

100% GRADUATE AND GO RIGHT INTO TEACHING

What's special

Dean's Statement

Cedarville's distinctly Christian, accredited early childhood education major will train teacher candidates to teach PreK–third grade in Christian or public schools. Early childhood majors take challenging coursework with a biblically integrated emphasis and participate in innovative field experiences during their teacher-training program. Teacher candidates will graduate ready to start their careers as compassionate Christian educators, ready to help students receive a strong education for lifelong learning and success. We believe that a degree in education is the opportunity to change lives for the Kingdom of God and at Cedarville, teacher candidates find plenty of ways to pursue their passions and hone their teaching skills: tutoring local students, teaching in area ministries, and educating diverse communities. Teacher candidates will have field experiences or clinical practice for both conventional and distance learning programs that provide experiences with PreK–third-grade students from different socioeconomic groups and ethnic/racial groups. Teacher candidates will also work with English language learners and students with disabilities during some of the field experiences and/or clinical practice to develop and practice the knowledge, skills, and professional dispositions for working with all students.

Where do candidates student teach?
- Xenia Community School District
- Legacy Christian Academy (Xenia, Ohio)
- Dayton City Schools

Campus Facts at a Glance

Size:	Medium
Location:	Town
Acceptance rate:	69%
Student to faculty ratio:	13 to 1
Graduation rate:	71%
Is education a top 5 major:	Yes

Financial

Tuition:	$28,110
In-state average annual cost:	$21,270
Students receiving federal loans:	49%
Typical debt:	$22,500

Typical Ohio new teacher salary:	**$33,096**

What's special about Cedarville University

Candidates' Observations

The professors in the School of Education at Cedarville University are incredible and go above and beyond. The professors care about you, not only academically but also about your life outside of the classroom.

Cedarville has a wonderful reputation, especially in the local schools we work with.

Stephanie Docter

Cedarville puts you in the classroom setting first off and I loved it. I loved being with kids every day and Cedarville did a good job of putting students in the classroom.

Brandon Williams

The professors provide a personal experience and they want to invest themselves in you and let you know that you are more than just an ID number.

Kami Gordon

Professors showed us by example what it means to respect others and our colleagues. They made us aware of the necessity of having a positive relationship with our mentor teachers, other teachers, our students, the principal, and other faculty and staff. We had a class specifically focused on having good communication with coworkers and parents. This class was hugely beneficial in learning practical and appropriate ways to communicate with and involve the parents of our students.

Megan Reed

I have really enjoyed my time in the TEP at Cedarville University. I have been challenged and equipped and I've seen myself grow. I enjoy education more now than I did before.

Victoria Molendyk

Clemson University
Clemson, SC

SCORE CARD
Secondary Indicators of Quality

Rigorous admissions process: **A**

Content preparation (social studies, science): **A**

High quality practice teaching: **C**

Learning to manage the classroom: **A**

90% (2014–2015) **90%** (2015–2016)
GRADUATE AND GO RIGHT INTO TEACHING

What's special

Dean's Statement

The secondary education program at Clemson University prepares students in English, mathematics, history, or science (physics, chemistry, biological sciences). Our students double major in secondary education and in their content area, all within four years. Multiple, diverse field experiences provide our students with opportunities to work with children from different ethnic, racial, gender, and socioeconomic groups and ultimately help prepare our students to excel in a myriad of educational settings. Our top-level faculty are recognized for their excellence in teaching, and we focus on engaging thought-provoking inquiry-based teaching and learning, intensive preparation in the content disciplines, ongoing interdisciplinary collaboration, and community outreach. Our secondary education program is one reason that we are "Best in Class" by striving for excellence, adhering to core values, and engaging our students in research and learning that prepares them to make a difference in the world.

Where do candidates student teach?
- Anderson County
- Greenville County
- Oconee County

Where do graduates work?
- Anderson County
- Greenville County
- Oconee County

Campus Facts at a Glance

Size:	Large
Location:	Suburban
Acceptance rate:	51%
Student to faculty ratio:	18 to 1
Graduation rate:	82%
Is education a top 5 major:	No

Financial

In-state tuition:	$14,708
Out-of-state tuition:	$34,590
In-state average annual cost:	$15,885
Students receiving federal loans:	43%
Typical debt:	$21,500

Typical South Carolina new teacher salary: **$32,306**

What's special about Clemson University

Candidates' Observations

The biggest strength of the Secondary program at Clemson University is the people. The professors and staff promote an environment of growth and improvement, encourage taking initiative, and provide individualized support for every student. I truly believe that the person I am today is because of the connections I have made with my professors at Clemson University. I would recommend this program to any aspiring educator who wants to be a part of a positive environment, which both challenges them and supports them while holding them to the highest standards. I feel incredibly prepared to begin my teaching career and I accredit that to the Clemson College of Education.

Secondary Education Student, Class of 2018

Clemson's Secondary Education program is made up of professors who practice what they preach and continuously model how to be a good educator. There has never been a moment where I have felt nervous to ask any of the professors for help because our success as students is undoubtedly their priority. Having professors who want you to grow, and will work with you on a Saturday morning to edit a lesson plan for a job interview, is something that makes our program so unique.

Secondary Education Student, Class of 2018

The secondary education program at Clemson University has been and continues to be a defining factor in molding me into a teacher. The program offers so much for its students, such as small courses where teachers can focus their time and energy on individual students, faculty and staff that believe in their students and in the program, and several resources, such as the Digital Media and Learning Lab, for students to use. The program allows you to become very close with the other students who were admitted at the same time as you. My cohort of students has become really close and I would consider some of them among my best friends. The program pushes collaboration, which is an important factor in any teacher's career. I recommend the secondary education program at Clemson University to any student who is looking for a collaborative learning environment with caring professors and innovative courses. This program truly is one of a kind.

Secondary Education Student, Class of 2019

Colorado Christian University
Lakewood, CO

SCORE CARD

Elementary Indicators of Quality		Secondary Indicators of Quality	
Rigorous admissions process:	A	Rigorous admissions process:	A
Learning how to teach reading:	A+	Content preparation (social studies, science):	A
Preparing to teach math:	B	High quality practice teaching:	C
High quality practice teaching:	C	Learning to manage the classroom:	A
Learning to manage the classroom:	A		

90% (2014–2015) 90% (2015–2016)
GRADUATE AND GO RIGHT INTO TEACHING

What's special

Dean's Statement – Elementary

Founded in 1914, Colorado Christian University is the premier interdenominational Christian university in Colorado and the eight-state Rocky Mountain region, delivering world-class education to thousands of students. The School of Education hosts state-approved licensure programs, with Elementary Education being the largest. Teaching has forever been a most personal enterprise, transpiring initially between two people in the crucible of questions like, "Who are we?", "Why are we here?" and "Where are we going?" These questions have traditionally formed the centerpiece of the teaching profession, helping us answer why we teach, what we teach, and how we teach. We build on that foundation with our professional education courses emphasizing rich content knowledge, rigorous pedagogical courses, a clinical teaching model in which students practice their teaching each year of their program, and experienced faculty with a deep commitment to helping our students be successful. We insist on quality partner schools, emphasizing exemplary preparation to teach reading and math using evidence-based practices. Finally, consistent with our commitment to preparing students with rich content knowledge, all of our elementary students graduate with a major in Liberal Arts, three 12-credit emphases in Social Studies, Reading and English Language Arts, and 39 credits in professional coursework.

Where do candidates student teach?
- Jefferson County School District
- Denver Public Schools
- Littleton Public Schools

Where do graduates work?
- Jefferson County School District
- Denver Public Schools
- Littleton Public Schools

Campus Facts at a Glance

Size:	Medium
Location:	City
Acceptance rate:	Info not available
Student to faculty ratio:	16 to 1
Graduation rate:	45%
Is education a top 5 major:	Yes

Financial

Tuition:	$29,360
In-state average annual cost:	$24,834
Students receiving federal loans:	49%
Typical debt:	$25,000
Typical Colorado new teacher salary:	**$32,126**

What's special about Colorado Christian University

Dean's Statement – Secondary

Founded in 1914, Colorado Christian University is the premier interdenominational Christian university in Colorado and the eight-state Rocky Mountain region, delivering world-class education to thousands of students. The School of Education hosts state-approved licensure programs, with Secondary Education being the second largest. Teaching has forever been a most personal enterprise, which transpires initially between two people in the crucible of questions like, "Who are we?", "Why are we here?" and "Where are we going?" These questions have traditionally formed the centerpiece of the teaching profession, helping us answer why we teach, what we teach, and how we teach. We build on that foundation with our professional education courses emphasizing rich content knowledge, rigorous pedagogical courses, a clinical teaching model in which students practice their teaching each year of their program, and experienced faculty with a deep commitment to helping our students be successful. We insist on quality partner schools and emphasize exemplary preparation to teach using evidence-based practices. Finally, consistent with our commitment to preparing students with rich content knowledge, all secondary students graduate with a 42+ credit major in their endorsement area (i.e., Social Studies, English, or General Science) and 36+ credits in SOE professional coursework.

Candidates' Observations – Elementary

The School of Education is a deeply rich program at CCU because it is one that calls upon passion and talent, while finessing skill and knowledge in a variety of content areas. This program is a gift to teacher candidates, like myself, who value authentic classroom experience and responsibility, while engaging in a self-reflective model of growth from day one that we can carry into our teaching careers. Thank you.

Sarah Cossick, *Class of 2017*

Teacher Candidate comments about their CCU Supervisors from the end-of-student teaching experience (May 2017):

- Kathy must have spent hours poring over my reflections and responding to every single one. In her responses she provided immense wisdom that comes from her level of experience. I sincerely appreciated the feedback she gave me, which allowed me to finesse my strengths and grow out of my weaknesses.

- Barb was wonderful. Every time she came into the classroom to observe she took the time to talk through it all with me and give me pointers. Specifically she helped me a great deal when it came to communication with my teacher. She helped make sure that we had good communication and were collaborating well.

- Lynn was incredibly intentional to point out specific things I did well and specific things I could work on. When there were things I needed to improve upon, such as differentiation, she willingly shared examples of how I can improve. As I prepared to create my Action Research Project unit, Lynn was quick to sit down with me and brainstorm instructional techniques, ideas, and concepts to incorporate into my lessons. She helped me to formulate the big picture of my unit and then break it down into tangible lessons.

School-Based Teacher who mentored one of our elementary teacher candidates in Jefferson County Schools (2017):

I just wanted to let you know how pleased I have been with my current Field I student, Juanita. She has been very organized, and she plans ahead, letting me know when she is switching observation dates a week ahead of schedule via phone call. I have been impressed with her rapport and interaction with the students. Juanita has always remained professional yet friendly, and she scaffolds students' questions with thoughtful, direct leading questions. Today, I told Juanita that I would teach a DLI lesson, then would allow her to teach the next day's lesson. I was incredibly impressed with how Juanita carried out the lesson. She varied her student participation, made clear the student expectations, and she asked great leading questions for students to think and respond to. Juanita was confident and poised throughout the lesson. She even did a brief review of the two concepts the kids had seemed to have difficulty with after the lesson was over. That initiative really set her apart. Aside from her demeanor with the kids and practice instruction, Juanita has been very reflective and open during our planning time. During our free time, Juanita has taken the initiative to ask me questions about when we plan, how long it takes (along with what I do) to plan for each lesson, along with what resources are available. To me, her questioning has made it clear that this is a profession she is truly invested and interested in. I know this email isn't necessarily needed for the program, but I wanted to reach out to let you know how wonderful this experience has been thus far with Juanita. She really seems to have a natural skill when it comes to teaching, and she's been great to work with!

What's special about Colorado Christian University

Candidates' Observations – Secondary

My supervisor was Amy Horton. One day when Mrs. Horton came to observe me, the lesson I taught did not go very well. When we were talking after, Mrs. Horton gave me some very honest feedback regarding my classroom management. While that was difficult to hear, it really made me think. The next lesson I taught as she observed went a lot better, and she praised my improvement.

Secondary Student, Class of 2017

See, what's different about CCU's Secondary Education Program is each professor and each piece of learning in every course is cultivated from, not only a deep passion for excellent education, but a specific calling to be an educator from God. Therefore, students who also receive this calling walk into the program and find their same exact heart, passion, and drive reflected back to them in just about everything. I remember walking out of my Field I class as a sophomore student, after presenting my first mock lesson to Professor John Borman and my fellow classmates feeling just pumped. That day the genuine encouragement and life-giving feedback I received further confirmed my calling to be a teacher and stoked the fire with an overflowing joy to pursue my future."

Meg Halloran
Class of 2016, just secured a secondary job
in Littleton Public Schools

When I entered into CCU's Secondary Education program in 2013, I was more than aware of the dropout rate for teachers entering the profession. I was daunted by the fact that teaching was a difficult profession. However, I am proud to say that four years later, I am thriving in my career choice. My classes at CCU prepared me for having my own classroom and my professors showed a true interest in building me up into the best educator I could be. I was supported throughout my time at CCU and was set up to thrive in classroom during my field experiences, student teaching, and life after college. I have true pride in my work, knowing I am making a difference and I know for certain that I made the right choice. Without the support along the way, I am not sure that would have been possible.

Cambria Magnuson-Raggio
Class of 2017, just secured a substitute teaching job
in Woodlands, Texas while applying for TX licensure through
reciprocity with Colorado

CUNY - Hunter College
New York, NY

SCORE CARD

Elementary Indicators of Quality		Secondary Indicators of Quality	
Rigorous admissions process:	A+	Rigorous admissions process:	A+
Learning how to teach reading:	D	Content preparation (social studies, science):	B/A
Preparing to teach math:	A	High quality practice teaching:	A
High quality practice teaching:	A	Learning to manage the classroom:	A
Learning to manage the classroom:	A		

77% TOTAL SINCE 2014
GRADUATE AND GO RIGHT INTO TEACHING

Where do candidates student teach?
- New York City Department of Education

Where do graduates work?
- New York City Department of Education
- NYC Charter Schools
- NYC Private Schools

Campus Facts at a Glance
Size:	Large
Location:	City
Acceptance rate:	38%
Student to faculty ratio:	11 to 1
Graduation rate:	53%
Is education a top 5 major:	No

Financial
In-state tuition:	$6,782
Out-of-state tuition:	$13,892
In-state average annual cost:	$7,742
Students receiving federal loans:	13%
Typical debt:	$11,548

Typical New York new teacher salary: **$43,839**

Dallas Baptist University
Dallas, TX

SCORE CARD
Elementary Indicators of Quality

Rigorous admissions process:	A
Learning how to teach reading:	C
Preparing to teach math:	A
High quality practice teaching:	C
Learning to manage the classroom:	A

80% (2014-2015) 83% (2015-16)
GRADUATE AND GO RIGHT INTO TEACHING

What's special

Dean's Statement

At Dallas Baptist University, we strongly believe only the best should be teachers, as the K-12 students in our country deserve nothing less. As a result, DBU has very high standards for admission, high expectations while training to be a teacher, and graduating only those who have the heart and the desire to make a difference in children's lives. For most of the teacher prep students at DBU, teaching is not just a great profession in which to work, but a "calling" that draws them to teaching. Our high standards are only exceeded by our students' desire to serve.

A hallmark of DBU's teacher preparation program is the emphasis on spending significant time in real K-12 classrooms. This begins when students are freshman and required to observe classrooms in local school districts. As a second semester junior and first semester senior, teacher prep students will enroll in "Field Experience" class spending two days a week in classrooms, not only observing but actually teaching and mentoring. After spending over 200 hours in the classroom already, second semester seniors will serve their schools five days a week for sixteen weeks in Clinical Teaching. By graduation, DBU students are ready to serve as experienced teachers.

Where do candidates student teach?
- Mansfield ISD
- Red Oak ISD
- Dallas ISD

Where do graduates work?
- Grand Prairie ISD
- Red Oak ISD
- Fort Worth ISD

Campus Facts at a Glance

Size:	Medium
Location:	City
Acceptance rate:	43%
Student to faculty ratio:	12 to 1
Graduation rate:	56%
Is education a top 5 major:	No

Financial

In-state tuition:	$26,180
In-state average annual cost:	$24,645
Students receiving federal loans:	62%
Typical debt:	$21,750
Typical Texas new teacher salary:	**$38,091**

What's special about Dallas Baptist University

Candidates' Observations

Dallas Baptist University's Education Program provides students with the opportunity to gain insight into the realities of the everyday classroom. In my time at DBU, the program has created an incomparable training ground that equips future educators with a mission- oriented focus: a mission to be the change in the classrooms, to create a place of exploration and discovery through brain-based learning, constructivist classroom setting, and hands on learning. What has made the most difference in my education, however, has been the heart of the professors. DBU has equipped me with the knowledge to become an educator, but what I have most treasured about the Education program has been the opportunity to have professors who care for me and want the absolute best for me, challenging me to exceed my expectations. To them I am not just another student, but rather they take time to invest and pour into me. There were quite a few instances when I would email Professor Oldenburg and ask to meet about one of my lessons, and together, we would sit in her office and go through my lesson line by line, talking through the strengths and weaknesses and how to best advance the instruction. Professor Hagan would begin class listening and allowing us the time to process and walk through our experiences in the classroom, sharing in our victories and encouraging us through the struggles while showing us how to apply it to our future classroom. They share their stories from being in the classroom and relate to us, celebrate our victories, and help overcome the small defeats. DBU professors care and have made an impact on my life that will far surpass my four years of college.

Alex Birkner

I would recommend the Dallas Baptist University College of Education to anyone looking to pursue a degree at any level of education. I would specifically highlight the Pedagogy of Science course in the degree plan. This course gives students authentic preparation in areas such as creating lesson plans, executing scientific investigation, and evaluating effectiveness. In addition to the Pedagogy of Science course, the College of Education at Dallas Baptist University excels at laying the groundwork for efficient and practical classroom management. In regards to professors in the Dallas Baptist University College of Education, the program has been blessed to obtain Christ-focused, loving, and intelligent leaders to prepare students for their future as teachers and outstanding leaders.

Blaire Kelley

I would recommend DBU's Education Preparation Program to anyone looking to become a teacher because I have seen and experienced the program's ability to prepare quality teachers who go above and beyond in the field of education. Our professors are dedicated to providing us with the best experience both inside and outside of the classroom. They are concerned with our personal lives and look for ways to mentor us as well as gearing classroom teaching towards our needs as students. The program's structure provides students with numerous hours of classroom experience and opportunities to learn from current teachers in the field which allows our students to feel prepared and comfortable in the classroom. Every Education course is interactive, collaborative, and creative. I have never once been in an Education class that was merely just a lecture. Every class provides us the opportunities to interact with our fellow classmates and professors to foster a collaborative and meaningful learning environment. I could go on and on about the quality of DBU's EPP, but the main indicator of its greatness is the kind of teachers it produces. I have seen my friends graduate from our program with excitement, passion, and confidence to be the best teachers they can be. Students from our program leave DBU with the experience to do their job well and the passion to change and improve the lives of students, colleagues, and families in their schools.

Bonnie Hatch

The excellence and thorough nature of the education programs is why I would recommend DBU to anyone pursuing to become an educator. The undergraduate DBU education programs excel in more areas than one, but the area that has most affected my time personally is the passion of professors. To have professors that have been passionate about the content they are teaching, students in schools we are reaching, and our teaching candidates has made all the difference. Professors in content areas I did not previously hold an interest in, particularly science, have not only made the content accessible, but relevant and interesting. With professors that I have constantly felt are in my corner, I now view content as important means to reach the hearts and minds of my future students. I could not have succeeded on a collegiate level or in a classroom without professors who have displayed passion in their teaching of our education courses.

Cara Miller

What's special about Dallas Baptist University

Candidates' Observations

After studying early childhood education at Dallas Baptist University, I am in awe of what I have learned and how prepared I feel to enter into the field of my dreams. My knowledge of best practices in education and professional pedagogy was once minute; now it is vast, and I owe it all to an incredible group of Christ-fearing servant leaders who have led me with their instruction. By cultivating my love for education, my professors have impacted me more than I could have ever imagined. DBU's Early Childhood Education Program is tough, but the results of such an intensive program are positive and extremely evident. Thanks to professors like Martha Neyland, Judy Abercrombie, and Patricia Davis, I know what it is like to be truly held accountable, incredibly encouraged, and intensely motivated to succeed. Not only have they shown me methods for effective instruction, they have truly modeled ways of exhibiting trustworthiness, loyalty, and love in the classroom; I know that, by following their examples, I will be able to maintain a safe and positive environment for my future students.

Haley Briggs

Going into college, many people around me fed me the idea that becoming an educator was somehow a decision to have a lesser career than what I was capable. This idea was quickly forgotten after I began my time at the Dallas Baptist University College of Education. As a member of the COE, I immediately felt encouraged, valued, and important.

One of the aspects that make the DBU program so distinguished is its professors. These professors are great, not just because they are well qualified to teach the content (which they are), but because each one is genuinely interested in the development of well-rounded, quality teachers. These professors want to see you succeed. My first experience in the COE came during my freshman orientation. The incoming students split up by major and I was able to sit in a room with all the people that would be starting this journey with me. Walking into the room, I was greeted by a huge group of professors and staff in the COE. Time was set apart to go around the room where we all introduced ourselves, said where we were from and talked about our dream teaching job. This time may not have seemed significant, but to me I immediately felt like I was joining something distinct and something special. My first education course that I was a part of was Introduction to Education with Professor Abercrombie. This class gave me a taste of what the rest of my time at DBU would entail and I loved it. After this class, I couldn't wait for more. Since then, I have had countless positive experiences with professors and other students. I have made so many great connections with people that I know will be there to support me when I move on from DBU and enter the classroom, and these connections are invaluable. I have grown so much as an educator and as a person because of the Dallas Baptist University College of Education and I wouldn't trade that for anything.

Natalie Jacquess

East Carolina University
Greenville, NC

SCORE CARD
Secondary Indicators of Quality
Rigorous admissions process:	**B**
Content preparation (social studies, science):	**A**
High quality practice teaching:	**B**
Learning to manage the classroom:	**B**

53% (TOTAL 2014-2016)
GRADUATE AND GO RIGHT INTO TEACHING

What's special

Dean's Statement

East Carolina University education students and graduates provide significant and far-reaching contributions to the schools, communities, and economies of North Carolina and beyond. Our programs are innovative and uniquely designed to effectively prepare candidates to improve student performance and to increase outcomes.

Where do candidates student teach?
- Pitt County
- Beaufort County
- Johnston County

Where do graduates work?
- Pitt County
- Wake County
- Johnston County

Campus Facts at a Glance
Size:	Large
Location:	City
Acceptance rate:	70%
Student to faculty ratio:	18 to 1
Graduation rate:	60%
Is education a top 5 major:	Yes

Financial
In-state tuition:	$6,997
Out-of-state tuition:	$22,955
In-state average annual cost:	$15,450
Students receiving federal loans:	56%
Typical debt:	$24,788
Typical North Carolina new teacher salary:	**$30,778**

Georgia College and State University
Milledgeville, GA

SCORE CARD
Elementary Indicators of Quality

Rigorous admissions process:	**A+**
Learning how to teach reading:	**B**
Preparing to teach math:	**D**
High quality practice teaching:	**C**
Learning to manage the classroom:	**C**

86% (2014-2015) **97%** (2015-2016)
GRADUATE AND GO RIGHT INTO TEACHING

What's special

Dean's Statement

Georgia College's elementary education program prepares you for a successful career as a distinguished teacher. Instead of large classes, as you enter our programs, you are teamed up to form a cohort and given a faculty mentor who will lead your group. You get to know your classmates and help each other throughout the program. We also have a tutoring system in place to support you if there is an area where you need a little extra assistance to be successful. Our academic advisors are there to meet with you personally and help you plan out your schedules. Our career counselors are also available throughout the program to assist you in developing yourself as a professional. In addition to the coursework, you participate in a variety of actual classrooms learning the successful ways to teach and manage students. In the end, your work pays off and you are most likely able to secure the teaching position of your choice. Since we are such a highly-respected program, school leaders across the state continuously contact us seeking to hire our graduates. Additionally, many of our graduates are teachers of the year throughout the state, another reflection of the quality of our program.

Dean, Dr. Joseph Peters

Where do candidates student teach?
- Baldwin County School District
- Jones County School District
- Putnam County School District

Where do graduates work?
- Bibb County School District
- Houston County School District
- Gwinnett County School District

Campus Facts at a Glance

Size:	Medium
Location:	Town
Acceptance rate:	85%
Student to faculty ratio:	17 to 1
Graduation rate:	61%
Is education a top 5 major:	Yes

Financial

In-state tuition:	$9,202
Out-of-state tuition:	$27,550
In-state average annual cost:	$17,283
Students receiving federal loans:	45%
Typical debt:	$22,000
Typical Georgia new teacher salary:	**$33,664**

What's special about Georgia College and State University

Candidates' Observations

There are many elements that make the Early Childhood program at Georgia College special. First, the program is divided into a cohort model. The cohort model places around 20 future educators in all the same classes throughout the two year program and they are all led by the same mentor. The mentor is the second element that I find special about this program. This mentor is a highly educated former educator that not only has the background knowledge of the best teaching practices and theory, but since they were former teachers, they have the ability to teach us from real life experiences. A third element in which I find special about the program at Georgia College is the time we spent in the field, hands-on teaching. During my two years in the program, I spent over 1,200 hours inside schools, with a host teacher, observing, planning, implementing, and reflecting multiple lessons. There are many more special elements of this program, but without those main three, I would not be the highly prepared teacher I am today.

Laurel Trust

The early childhood education program at Georgia College is so special because it really is like a family. Your cohort leaders and professors genuinely care about your success and want to help you become the best teacher possible, and the girls in my cohort have become some of my closest friends who have supported me through all the ups and downs that come with being a college student in one of the most rigorous programs on campus. We have so much experience in the classroom, not just observing but actually teaching that I feel like I'll be fully prepared to have my own classroom next year. Helping our students is at the root of everything we do, and making sure they are safe and happy and healthy is priority above all else.

Elena Campfield

The extensive hours of field-based practicums that are required throughout the Early Childhood program have given me the opportunity to witness the powerful reality of my own education in the education of the students that I teach. The program is intentionally structured to provide you with the unique experience of truly becoming an educator.

Jessica Capo

The Georgia College Early Childhood program is unique because of its commitment to preparing pre-service teachers to best excel in the education field through an in depth analysis of child development and education theories. This program refuses to simply follow the traditional authoritarian-led teaching model, but rather, this program challenges pre-service teachers to look beyond the traditional classroom and imagine an environment where each child feels empowered, protected, capable, and loved.

Caroline Minter

The Georgia College Early Childhood Education Program is outstanding because of the hands-on experiences provided in elementary school classrooms. I started working with teachers and classroom mentors at the beginning of my college experience. This allowed me to build peer and teacher relationships and also work directly with children. The program provides a wonderful mentor led experience through our cohort style classes. The cohort classes offer a personal approach to learning, and I have gained the confidence necessary to one day reach my professional goals.

Katherine Hunt

Why would you recommend this program to people who are looking to become a teacher?

I would recommend this program to anyone who is looking to become a teacher due to my overall experience. The mentor leader and professors I had expected me to go above and beyond what was expected in order to be the best teacher for my students. By being in the field as many hours as we were, I was able to know my students personally and academically. This helped me guide my instruction in order to best teach my students. Without this program, I would not be as prepared for teaching in my own classroom as I am now.

Laurel Trust

Gordon College
Wenham, MA

SCORE CARD
Secondary Indicators of Quality

Rigorous admissions process:	**A**
Content preparation (social studies, science):	**A**
High quality practice teaching:	**C**
Learning to manage the classroom:	**B**

78% (2014–2015) **76%** (2015–2016)
GRADUATE AND GO RIGHT INTO TEACHING

What's special

Dean's Statement

Teacher education has been at the core of Gordon College's mission since its founding more than 125 years ago. Our students engage in a rigorous liberal arts education in conjunction with hands-on experience in both the art and science of teaching. Our faculty invest in their students through deep mentoring outside of the classroom and setting high expectations within. The work ethic exhibited by our students is a hallmark of our programs, and it undergirds the strong partnerships we maintain with school systems throughout the region. Teaching is about helping young people to grow both inside and out. We take seriously our calling to empower our students to make a difference in the lives of their students.

Sandra Doneski, PhD
Dean of Faculty, Gordon College

Where do candidates student teach?
- Danvers, MA
- Gloucester, MA
- Masconomet District

Where do graduates work?
- Gloucester, MA
- Lynnfield, MA
- Lynn, MA

Campus Facts at a Glance

Size:	Small
Location:	Suburban
Acceptance rate:	92%
Student to faculty ratio:	12 to 1
Graduation rate:	71%
Is education a top 5 major:	No

Financial

Tuition:	$36,060
In-state average annual cost:	$27,418
Students receiving federal loans:	69%
Typical debt:	$27,000

Typical Massachusetts new teacher salary: **$40,600**

What's special about Gordon College

Candidates' Observations

I would recommend this program to upcoming teachers because our professors are not only extremely knowledgeable in their field but have many years of practice in the field themselves. They answer all of your questions quickly and in depth and usually share a personal story of their own! You always feel prepared going into the schools for observations/teaching and the professors are very easy to talk to if you need help. Overall, there's no other place I'd rather be studying education and no other team of professors I'd rather be studying under.

Like all teachers, the first year (well, first three years if we're being honest) was a lot of work and a major learning curve, but I felt very well prepared. I have found that everything we covered in the program was one step ahead of the initiatives my school has been taking, continuing to set me apart as a knowledgeable and prepared professional. This includes higher order thinking, differentiation, lesson planning, understanding by design, and so much more.

Thinking back on my experience at Gordon, I am so thankful for the support of my professors and advisers. My student teaching experience at a Boston Public School was extremely challenging and it was not what I expected. Whenever I felt like I had failed or hit an impossible obstacle, my professors were so willing to listen to my struggles and provide practical suggestions stemming from their experience with classroom management and student engagement. But most importantly, they encouraged me to never give up on my students and hold high expectations with the belief that my students could and would learn.

I am currently working at Mystic Valley Regional Charter School in Malden, MA as a floater teacher and am so thankful for the education that Gordon gave me. I feel more than prepared to step into any given classroom and feel confident. Gordon has challenged me and grown me so much as a teacher and a person. The professors I was blessed to have at Gordon gave me more feedback and help than their job required. They truly went above and beyond to ensure that I would be a great teacher and I think I am well on the road to that end goal thanks to the Gordon Education program. To anyone considering Gordon's Education program, I would strongly recommend it as you will be put into situations where you are well supported and challenged to become the best teacher you can possibly be.

I would recommend Gordon because it allows for its students to access schools at an early beginning. Gordon's full immersion [via field lab] into local school districts in the first year helped to inspire my drive to be a quality teacher. My professors at Gordon challenged me to be my best, while making sure I am cared for and seeing that students are thriving.

I would recommend this program to people who are looking to become a teacher because the faculty and staff are awesome. They share valuable first-hand experience and insight from their time in the field, and truly want to set you up for success in your future classroom.

Henderson State University
Arkadelphia, AR

SCORE CARD
Elementary Indicators of Quality

Rigorous admissions process:	**B**
Learning how to teach reading:	**D**
Preparing to teach math:	**A**
High quality practice teaching:	**C**
Learning to manage the classroom:	**B**

What's special

Candidates' Observations

I have grown so much through the program, in myself and as a future teacher. The instructors are student focused, and the intimate class size fosters healthy faculty student relationships. I know that when I graduate, I will have not just one but a set of mentors invested in me and my career.

Emily Wetzlar

Our Elementary Education program at Henderson State Teacher's College is statewide and nationally recognized because of the superior (teaching) quality our professors demonstrate. Our program guarantees that every teacher candidate possesses the six dispositions (caring for students and their families, sensitivity to diversity, sense of fairness, sense of efficacy, personal reflection, and sense of professionalism) to be a successful educator. In addition, our faculty exhibits the same dispositions to each candidate to represent our program's expectations and model how we should exhibit these same dispositions in the classroom to possess high quality as a teacher. Our faculty and program ensure that we have real-world experiences when we graduate and are familiar with all the newest technology to educate tomorrows future leaders effectively. Our elementary education program prepares our teaching candidates how to apply strategies, plan lessons and units, implement technology into developmentally appropriate instruction, and apply real-world experiences to effectively teach a diverse group of learners in the twenty-first-century classroom.

Corey Jackson
Class of 2018

Campus Facts at a Glance

Size:	Medium
Location:	Town
Acceptance rate:	66%
Student to faculty ratio:	16 to 1
Graduation rate:	35%
Is education a top 5 major:	Yes

Financial

In-state tuition:	$8,340
Out-of-state tuition:	$15,180
In-state average annual cost:	$9,937
Students receiving federal loans:	61%
Typical debt:	$19,500
Typical Arkansas new teacher salary:	**$32,691**

High Point University

High Point, NC

SCORE CARD

Elementary Indicators of Quality	
Rigorous admissions process:	A+
Learning how to teach reading:	A
Preparing to teach math:	F
High quality practice teaching:	A
Learning to manage the classroom:	C

Secondary Indicators of Quality	
Rigorous admissions process:	A
Content preparation (social studies, science):	A/C
High quality practice teaching:	A
Learning to manage the classroom:	C

95% (2014-2015) **81%** (2015-2016) IN ELEMENTARY
100% (2014-2015) **75%** (2015-2016) IN SECONDARY
GRADUATE AND GO RIGHT INTO TEACHING

What's special

Dean's Statement – Elementary

Today's teacher preparation programs should equip graduates with the knowledge and skills to create learning environments that allow students to succeed in life, career, and citizenship. The mission of our elementary education program is to produce great teachers who do not just simply "do" the job of teaching, but are continuously challenged to think about what they are doing, why they are doing it, and how to adapt when desired outcomes are not achieved. Clinical field experiences begin in the freshman year and conclude with a full year of student teaching. Historically, the School of Education has enjoyed many collaborative partnerships with area elementary schools and recently expanded these to include business stakeholders such as LEGO Education North America. LEGO Education at High Point University is an outreach program that has hosted more than 8,000 children in grades 3-8 for STEM events and summer enrichment camps. Elementary education majors may apply for admission to the B.A. to M.Ed. program in their senior year and can specialize in advanced coursework in STEM, Robotics, or Literacy leading to the master's degree in Elementary Education.

(continued on next page)

Where do candidates student teach?

- Guilford County Schools
- Davidson County Schools
- Winston Salem-Forsyth County Schools

Where do graduates work?

- Guilford County Schools: North Carolina
- Davidson County Schools

Campus Facts at a Glance

Size:	Medium
Location:	City
Acceptance rate:	79%
Student to faculty ratio:	15 to 1
Graduation rate:	64%
Is education a top 5 major:	Yes

Financial

Tuition:	$33,405
In-state average annual cost:	$37,219
Students receiving federal loans:	44%
Typical debt:	$22,422
Typical North Carolina new teacher salary:	**$30,778**

What's special about High Point University

Dean's Statement – Elementary

To ensure continued success, the School of Education's commitment to our students does not end with May graduation. The *Mentor Teacher Program* utilizes retired teachers and faculty who provide face-to-face or virtual coaching and professional development. Since 2013, 89% of our graduates in elementary education have remained in the teaching profession beyond their first three years of teaching.

Dean's Statement – Secondary

Students completing Secondary Education programs of study at High Point University major in the content areas of Mathematics, Biology, English or History/Social Studies within the College of Arts and Sciences. Faculty within each of these disciplines serve as liaisons to the School of Education to ensure that those seeking 9-12 licensure meet both their major and education requirements. Coursework offered through the Stout School of Education includes required educational coursework as well as significant opportunities for service learning, study abroad and undergraduate research. The Stout School of Education uses qualified clinical educators in collaboration with our full time faculty to deliver all secondary education programs. The student teaching internship is paired with methodology courses that are taught by clinical faculty in their own classrooms, thus integrating an experience that combines exposure to teaching methodologies with continued opportunity for practice. At the conclusion of the program, secondary education majors may choose to apply for admission into the B.A. to M.Ed. program and can enroll in up to three graduate level courses leading to the advanced degree in Educational Leadership. Within this track, additional school or community-based internships, conference presentations and other activities designed to shape teacher leadership skills are emphasized.

Candidates' Observations – Elementary

When deciding to attend High Point University as a high school senior, my influence was heavily based on all that was offered through the Elementary Education program. I knew I had wanted to be a teacher since I was in elementary school so the rigor in courses, encouraging staff and overall experience based learning solidified that High Point University's School of Education would help me become the best teacher I could possibly be.

Ms. Claudia Beard, *Class of 2017*
Elementary Education
2017 North Carolina Student Teacher of the Year Nominee
Cornerstone Charter Academy of Greensboro, NC, August 2017

As a result of her teaching, Dr. Disseler has shown all future teachers what it means to be "all in" for their students...she has pushed me to develop a passion for teaching and foster an even deeper love for learning. Dr. Disseler has pushed me to take risks, and cultivate my talents as a leader and teacher. It is because of these attributes that I, along with many of my peers, are where we are today in terms of our career and growth as individuals.

Ms. Rachel Lawrence, *Class of 2012*
Middle Grades Education Math/Science: Wake County Schools, NC
Kenan Fellow: Kenan Institute of Engineering, Technology &
Science, 2016 Emerging Young Leader by ASCD

In the start of the second semester of my junior year, little did I know that I was about to meet the person I would hope to some day become. For the past three years I have had the sincere pleasure of being a student in Dr. Disseler's class. Every class I have had with her I have been engaged while learning the most up-to-date teaching pedagogy, and most importantly, learning how to become the best teacher I can be. Dr. Disseler's drive for success is incomparable. She always makes time for others and offers her help with an open ear and an open heart. She has taught me that failure is just a part of the journey, and how to come out of these failures even stronger with a willingness to succeed. When I think about who I want to eventually become, my mind goes straight to Dr. Disseler. She has left an imprint on who I am as a person, and I am forever thankful for the significant impact she has made on me as a student, teacher, colleague, and life-long friend.

Ms. Taylor Niss, *Class of 2017*
North Brevard Prep School STEM
Fort Lauderdale, Fla.

What's special about High Point University

Candidates' Observations – Elementary

The faculty in the Stout School of Education is always looking ahead of the curve. They understand when their students get into the field upon graduation that the playing field is going to be completely different than it is today. They take this into consideration and prepare you to be ready when it comes time to enter your very first classroom.

Mr. Chris Tertzigni, *Class of 2014*
Elementary Education, Northeast Middle School, Guilford County Schools

Candidates' Observations – Secondary

The Educator Preparation program at HPU has given me opportunities to be in the classroom since freshman year. Because of this, I have been able to experience different school cultures than what I was used to. I went to a private school my whole life and had my first public school exposure during my freshman year at HPU. This experience helped me decide that I want to teach in a public school one day. The teachers within the Stout School of Education at High Point University have given me guidance and have been prime examples of the supportive teacher that I want to become.

Hailey Adair
Senior, Secondary Math 9-12

In one of my courses on Literacy in the Content Areas, my education professor, Dr. Albritton, assigned a literacy project in which we were required to write a chapter for a textbook, illustrating both a mastery of our subject and the best features of instructional text. That project allowed me to focus on the literacy aspects specific to my content area, history. I developed a new appreciation for how reading varies from discipline to discipline, and how teaching must also vary in order to connect that discipline with students. It was a great assignment.

Grant Johnson
Senior, Secondary History/Social Studies 9-12

My time spent at High Point University's School of Education has prepared me for my first year of teaching many times over. I thank God that I was able to have the opportunity to work with faculty and staff who were always available to me as I honed my professional skills and character traits in order to develop into the teacher that I wanted to be. During my time at High Point University I was able to gain experience through multiple internships and teaching experiences, which I believe played a big role in me being able to acquire my first teaching position.

Hannah Wiley, *Class of 2017*
Secondary Education: 9-12 (Mathematics)
Westchester Academy High Point

Hope College
Holland, MI

SCORE CARD

Secondary Indicators of Quality

Rigorous admissions process: **A**

Content preparation (social studies, science): **A**

High quality practice teaching: **C**

Learning to manage the classroom: **A**

85% (2014–2015) **93%** (2015–2016)
GRADUATE AND GO RIGHT INTO TEACHING

What's special

Dean's Statement

Four important elements make the Hope College Education Department unique in preparing future secondary teachers. First, classes are small, rarely exceeding 25 students per section and are usually even smaller. Second, every student in every course participates in a field placement. This opportunity for experiential learning links theory to practice in a way that makes course knowledge come alive and prepares future teachers for life in the classroom. Third, faculty members are current in the most recent theory, research, and practice. They conduct original research, publish articles and books, and present at national and international conferences. They are leaders in their field. They spend time in classrooms doing research and partnering with current teachers. This work keeps them on the cutting edge of theory, research and practice, which trickles down to our students. Fourth, Hope is a liberal arts college, so students in the teacher education program leave Hope with more than just knowledge about how to be excellent teachers. They also take courses outside of the education department that cultivate skills in reading, writing, analysis, and ethical decision-making. It is very rare to have all four of these important elements present in a teacher education program. Hope does.

Dr. Scott VanderStoep
Dean for Social Sciences, Hope College

Where do candidates student teach?
- West Ottawa Public Schools
- Holland Public Schools
- Zeeland Public Schools

Where do graduates work?
- Holland Public Schools
- Hamilton Community Schools
- Zeeland Public Schools

Campus Facts at a Glance

Size: Medium

Location: City

Acceptance rate: 84%

Student to faculty ratio: 11 to 1

Graduation rate: 78%

Is education a top 5 major: Yes

Financial

Out-of-state tuition: $31,560

In-state average annual cost: $23,994

Students receiving federal loans: 55%

Typical debt: $27,000

Typical Michigan new teacher salary: **$35,901**

What's special about Hope College

Candidates' Observations

To me, the faculty within Hope's education department make the program incredibly rich. Their expertise, encouragement, and embodiment of core teaching values are the building blocks of pre-service teacher education. Two particularly influential professors throughout my time at Hope have been Professor William Moreau and Dr. Deborah Van Duinen. Both of them have instilled an excitement for secondary teaching in me, as well as the endurance to push beyond my limits. Due to Professor Moreau's English Methods course, I gained the ability to thoroughly plan in my content area while extensively building up my resources for teaching English. Dr. Van Duinen, through class and summer research, inspired me to constantly evolve my teaching practices to keep up with dynamic classroom pedagogy. Without these two individuals, I would not be the passionate and driven individual that I am, striving to emulate their approach at teaching young people.

Brookelyn Wharton

Having applied to the teacher education program was the best decision I have made in my time at Hope. Through it I have grown so much as a person and a future educator. I am thankful for all the help I have received, but especially thankful for John Yelding who has been by my side through all the doubts and bumps. I am thankful for him for not only being a mentor but also a second father figure. Being a first generation student is not easy and having a connection with someone in the department who understands has been the reason for my success and motivation to continue throughout all the times I wished to just go home.

Lizette Barona

Hope College's department of education has had a large influence on my life as an educator and person. Not only does the program offer real, practical field experiences prior to student teaching, it also presents its students with genuine faculty and staff. In particular, as a music education major, Dr. Christina Hornbach helped guide me through a lot of my time at Hope. She helped me see the holistic image of teaching and understand that all experiences make us better educators. She did this not only through her work and advice but also through her genuine intentionality. When I met with her while a student, it wasn't always academically centered and often took place at a coffee shop. As a result of the relationship I formed with Dr. Hornbach while at Hope, I know that I will continue to stay in touch with her as a resource and friend long beyond Hope.

Hilary Hunsberger

Lewis-Clark State College
Lewiston, ID

SCORE CARD
Elementary Indicators of Quality

Rigorous admissions process:	C
Learning how to teach reading:	D
Preparing to teach math:	C
High quality practice teaching:	C
Learning to manage the classroom:	B

95% (2014-2015) 90% (2015-2016)
GRADUATE AND GO RIGHT INTO TEACHING

What's special

Dean's Statement

Lewis-Clark State College fosters student passion for education and teaching excellence by integrating theory and practice throughout the education curriculum. Elementary education majors are placed in real school classrooms almost from the beginning of their college careers, from early practicums to field experiences to a culminating full-year teaching internship prior to graduation and certification. During their college career, elementary education majors are supported to achieve their academic and career goals with highly-effective instruction and individualized mentoring by college faculty and partner-school classroom teachers. Elementary Education majors graduate from Lewis-Clark State College well-prepared for their first teaching position and ready to participate in educating and empowering students to achieve their own dreams.

Mary Flores
Dean for Academic Programs

Where do candidates student teach?
- Lewiston Independent School District No. 1 (ID)
- Post Falls School District No. 273 (ID)
- Clarkston School District (WA)

Where do graduates work?
- Lewiston Independent School District No. 1
- Post Falls School District No. 273
- Coeur d'Alene School District

Campus Facts at a Glance

Size:	Medium
Location:	City
Acceptance rate:	97%
Student to faculty ratio:	14 to 1
Graduation rate:	29%
Is education a top 5 major:	Yes

Financial

In-state tuition:	$6,120
Out-of-state tuition:	$17,620
In-state average annual cost:	$14,916
Students receiving federal loans:	44%
Typical debt:	$21,944

**Typical Idaho
new teacher salary:** **$31,159**

What's special about Lewis-Clark State College

Candidates' Observations

The Elementary Education Program at Lewis-Clark State (LCSC) is truly a one-of-a-kind program. From the moment you enter the program, you are directed into the most fulfilling two years of your lifetime. With the guidance of a faculty who specialize in a variety of academics, you are set on the path to becoming a great educator. You learn the foundational skills it takes to be an effective educator in today's world while also learning tactics and techniques that set LCSC teaching candidates apart from any others. You are put in connection with all different types of students, teachers, and community mentors who help strengthen your skills and push you to do your absolute best. The experiences you have in the Education Program are truly life-changing and will benefit you during every step of the way towards becoming an educator.

Arianne J. Hartley
4th Grade Teacher, McSorley Elementary, Lewiston, Idaho

Lewis-Clark State College has an outstanding program for people who want to become teachers. Before I came to LCSC I had taken some education classes at a different college. These classes were good but nothing compared to the ones that I took at LCSC. The education classes provided a lot of experience in classrooms and taught lessons that you could see and use during the times in the classroom. All the education staff are very friendly and helpful. Often, they went out of the way to make sure that you had all the help that you need and to see if they could help you beyond the classroom. At LCSC, you will also have the chance to do a year-long internship in two classrooms. This longer internship provided me with not only experience but created lifelong relationships and mentors.

Jasmine Smith

I would recommend LCSC's program to anyone and I do all the time. It is the best teacher prep program because it is so intense and prepares you for what's to come. I remember someone telling me once that first year teachers from LCSC are not as overwhelmed as other college grads because they already have the year-long intern experience and know more of what to expect. Although the program is extremely intense, it is also supported by professors who care and make themselves available at all times. There are so many great things about LCSC. It was an honor and a privilege to graduate from their program.

Dani Bozzuto

I would recommend the LCSC Teacher Education Program to anyone who is looking to become a teacher for several different reasons. First, the faculty and staff work to build a relationship with you. I never felt like I was being "taught" from my professors, it was more of a 4-year "training" service. I was amazed to go to class, walk around campus, or walk into the education office and be greeted with my name! It blew my mind! Plus, we laughed together, we were mad together, and we cried together. To have a college professor sit and listen to your stresses or even cry with you is unreal and it builds a phenomenal relationship! Secondly, as I said above, the LCSC Teacher Education Program is so fortunate to have amazing elementary school staff across the valley that are so willing to allow students to train and observe them in their classroom day in and day out. Principals and administrators from around the region know when they see an LCSC student or graduate because they are ready to teach and prepared to do so. Lastly, I love LCSC because after you graduate, the faculty and staff aren't just someone in your past. They stick alongside you for your journey into your new career. They WANT to be used as a resource! They WANT to be kept in the loop on how your teaching "gig" is going! And most importantly, they WANT you to know that you are supported by them every step of the way so that you, like them, can have a positive impact in these children's lives!

Dustin Wendt
5th/6th Grade Teacher, Grantham Elementary School, Lewiston, Idaho

LCSC's Teacher Education Program ensures that new educators are equipped with the tools and in-class experiences to begin teaching right away. The professors and faculty expect the highest performances from their teacher candidates. One professor told our class that he would only pass us if he felt comfortable enrolling his children in our classrooms. This stuck with me, and made me realize the expectation LCSC holds for their graduates. I feel very fortunate to have gone through such a strong, well-known program.

Elizabeth Quinley
Pullman School District

Lipscomb University
Nashville, TN

SCORE CARD
Secondary Indicators of Quality

Rigorous admissions process:	**A+**
Content preparation (social studies, science):	**A**
High quality practice teaching:	**A**
Learning to manage the classroom:	**A**

98% (2014–2015) **98%** (2015–2016)
GRADUATE AND GO RIGHT INTO TEACHING

What's special

Dean's Statement

Each of us can name a teacher whose influence changed our lives. That teacher's excitement about math or chemistry was contagious. That teacher made literature or music or history come to life for us. We fell in love with physics or drama or cross-country track because of that teacher's influence. Whatever it was, we were forever changed because a teacher opened the door and connected us to our potential. The goal of Lipscomb's teacher prep program is to build prospective teachers ready to become life-changers in today's PK-12 schools. Through academics and service, students in Lipscomb's program connect life and learning. They build knowledge and skills, develop relationships and attitudes, and work alongside faculty and colleagues to practice and refine teaching as art and science. Located in the heart of Nashville, Lipscomb offers prospective teachers the opportunity to work with educators and students from richly varied backgrounds during extensive practical experiences in diverse partner schools, both public and private, in an engaging and challenging academic environment. As a career, teaching is life changing. It offers the opportunity of opening endless possibilities for students, and its greatest reward lies in changing the lives of generations to come.

Where do candidates student teach?
- Metro Nashville Public Schools
- Sumner County Schools
- Rutherford County Schools

Where do graduates work?
- Metro Nashville Public Schools
- Sumner County Schools
- Williamson County Schools

Campus Facts at a Glance

Size:	Medium
Location:	City
Acceptance rate:	61%
Student to faculty ratio:	12 to 1
Graduation rate:	59%
Is education a top 5 major:	Yes

Financial

Tuition:	$29,756
In-state average annual cost:	$24,560
Students receiving federal loans:	53%
Typical debt:	$20,500
Typical Tennessee new teacher salary:	**$34,098**

What's special about Lipscomb University

Candidates' Observations

I would recommend this program because (I am confident that) Lipscomb's College of Education equips its students with the tools to be an effective (communicator, listener, leader and) teacher. The program emphasizes student based lessons and uses updated research to support pedagogy and instruction. I've learned about who I want to be as a teacher, staff member, and as a servant leader in my future school community. Lipscomb has taught me about how to help my students reach their full potential through helping me realize mine. The Lipscomb faculty invests in their students and goes above and beyond to encourage their full potential. They are the best of the best; they are master teachers. I'm leaving undergrad motivated and eager to get started and I'm thankful for the faculty for investing in me and encouraging me along the way.

Louisiana Tech University
Ruston, LA

SCORE CARD
Elementary Indicators of Quality

Rigorous admissions process: **A**
Learning how to teach reading: **B**
Preparing to teach math: **A**
High quality practice teaching: **B**
Learning to manage the classroom: **B**

73% (2014-2015) **73%** (2015-2016)
GRADUATE AND GO RIGHT INTO TEACHING

What's special

Candidates' Observations

The first weeks of school have been more than I could ever ask for in my life. Never have I been more sure of the profession I want to join. These weeks have given me courage and strength and a new place to call my home. I feel like I'm part of an amazing school. My grade level team acknowledges me as one of them. I have input in the lessons and opinions.

Laura Davidson, *2015-2016 Intern*

The advantages to participating in the clinical residency all year are endless! The full-year clinical residency allows me to experience so many things: if a new student comes, if a student fights, if the 8-week unit becomes a 10-week unit, when a 5th grader reads on a 1st grade reading level, and so many more. I'm learning teaching skills daily just being there.

Dana Reno, *2015-2016 Intern*

There are countless advantages to this program. Let's start with the fact that I have become so knowledgeable in the first week of school. I feel I will be more prepared to start a job right after I graduate.

Laura Davidson, *2015-2016 Intern*

Where do candidates student teach?
- Lincoln Parish School District
- Monroe City Parish District School District
- Ouachita Parish School District

Where do graduates work?
- Lincoln Parish School District
- Bossier Parish School District
- Caddo Parish School District

Campus Facts at a Glance
Size: Medium
Location: Town
Acceptance rate: 63%
Student to faculty ratio: 24 to 1
Graduation rate: 52%
Is education a top 5 major: No

Financial
In-state tuition: $9,117
Out-of-state tuition: $25,851
In-state average annual cost: $9,233
Students receiving federal loans: 30%
Typical debt: $19,865

**Typical Louisiana
new teacher salary:** **$38,655**

Marshall University

Huntington, WV

SCORE CARD

Elementary Indicators of Quality

Rigorous admissions process:	A
Learning how to teach reading:	A
Preparing to teach math:	B
High quality practice teaching:	D
Learning to manage the classroom:	B

75% (2014-2015) **75%** (2015-2016)
GRADUATE AND GO RIGHT INTO TEACHING

What's special

Dean's Statement

Marshall University's Elementary Education Program is the premier program for teacher preparation in our region. Our teacher candidates are out in area schools throughout the majority of their programs, gaining experience and insight into the profession and into their own skills and interests. The number of hours our students spend in real school settings goes beyond state and national requirements. The program is large enough to provide a wide set of experiences, while small enough to give our students personal attention and valuable guidance.

Students experience a strong program in early reading training, a key component in successful teaching. While completing our elementary education program, students have the option of adding on experiences in early childhood education and/or multi-categorical special education to make them eligible for endorsements to enhance their career opportunities.

Both the Early Childhood and Elementary Education programs are recognized on a national level. A significant percentage of the students in local districts are graduates of Marshall's teacher preparation program. Area superintendents and personnel directors are always anxious to hire our graduates.

Where do candidates student teach?

- Cabell County Schools
- Wayne County Schools
- Putnam County Schools

Where do graduates work?

- Cabell County Schools
- Wayne County Schools
- Putnam County Schools

Campus Facts at a Glance

Size:	Medium
Location:	City
Acceptance rate:	89%
Student to faculty ratio:	19 to 1
Graduation rate:	45%
Is education a top 5 major:	Yes

Financial

In-state tuition:	$7,154
Out-of-state tuition:	$16,382
In-state average annual cost:	$9,508
Students receiving federal loans:	59%
Typical debt:	$23,135
Typical West Virginia new teacher salary:	**$32,533**

What's special about Marshall University

Candidates' Observations

I believe that Marshall has one of the best teaching programs because of the professors. They genuinely care about your education and are willing to make your dreams and goals a reality.

Maddy

Everybody here knows everybody. It's easy to find someone who knows the answers to your questions. I've had situations where I needed help, and I've been able to find it.

Kayla

Marshall University's COEPD is not just a college, it's a family. Professors know your name and sincerely care about your success.

Taylor

Milligan College
Milligan College, TN

SCORE CARD

Secondary Indicators of Quality

Rigorous admissions process:	**A**
Content preparation (social studies, science):	**A**
High quality practice teaching:	**D**
Learning to manage the classroom:	**A**

What's special

Candidates' Observations

I like how detailed classes are within the education program. We focus on all aspects of education, which prepares us for work in the schools. I also like the relationships with professors and the smaller classes, which help us dig deeper into content.

Savannah Raizor

I've gained more experience in the classroom and have more knowledge about how to be a successful teacher in the future.

Taylor Fleming

Milligan's Education Program was one of the biggest reasons I chose to go to Milligan. The reputation the program has is something that really attracted me to Milligan. Without the program, I wouldn't be where I am today. I graduated from Milligan on May 6th and by May 24th had a teaching job, and I believe this was because of the education program. The professors are phenomenal, so personable, and did everything they could to prepare me for a teaching position. I am forever grateful for Milligan's Education Program, my professors, and for the endless encouragement I received while in the program.

Jadin Graham

Campus Facts at a Glance

Size:	Small
Location:	Suburban
Acceptance rate:	72%
Student to faculty ratio:	10 to 1
Graduation rate:	63%
Is education a top 5 major:	No

Financial

Tuition:	$31,450
In-state average annual cost:	$19,114
Students receiving federal loans:	57%
Typical debt:	$25,500
Typical Tennessee new teacher salary:	**$34,098**

Mississippi College
Clinton, MS

SCORE CARD
Elementary Indicators of Quality

Rigorous admissions process:	**B**
Learning how to teach reading:	**A**
Preparing to teach math:	**A**
High quality practice teaching:	**D**
Learning to manage the classroom:	**Not reviewed**

94% (2014-2015) **94%** (2015-2016)
GRADUATE AND GO RIGHT INTO TEACHING

What's special

Dean's Statement

Our program is widely known for its strong academic reputation and commitment to excellence, and has been nationally accredited for more than sixty years. With small university class sizes, our professors truly get to know our students and work closely with them to build their teaching and classroom preparation skills, as well as provide highly personalized job recommendations for our graduates.

Our program provides candidates with a plethora of very diverse field experiences throughout the program. Logging well over 600 hours in supervised K-6 classroom settings before they even graduate from our program, candidates spend time in various grade levels, subject areas, classrooms, communities, and school districts. Field experiences begin during the sophomore year, and each semester candidates spend time in different classrooms experiencing many types of learners, teachers, families, communities, and administrators. Additionally, our program provides up-to-date preparation on technology, methodologies, and instruction, as well as research and evidence based learning and teaching strategies for all learners. Teacher candidates leave our program with the knowledge, skills, dispositions, integrity, and compassion to make a difference in the field of elementary education.

Where do candidates student teach?
- Jackson Public Schools
- Madison County Schools
- Clinton Public School District

Where do graduates work?
- Clinton Public School District
- Rankin County Public School District
- Hinds County Public School District

Campus Facts at a Glance

Size:	Medium
Location:	Suburban
Acceptance rate:	49%
Student to faculty ratio:	15 to 1
Graduation rate:	54%
Is education a top 5 major:	Yes

Financial

Tuition:	$16,740
In-state average annual cost:	$15,375
Students receiving federal loans:	54%
Typical debt:	$25,000
Typical Mississippi new teacher salary:	**$31,184**

What's special about Mississippi College

Candidates' Observations

I'm a big believer in learning from practitioners. The faculty, both leading the program and teaching the courses, were really high-quality people. That meant a lot to me.

DeSean Dyson
HeadMaster, The Redeemer's School, Jackson, Mississippi

Mississippi College has an excellent Teacher Education program where each professor is interested in my success. I am a better teacher because they have invested their time and shared their expertise with me.

Dr. Myra Kinchen
first grade teacher, Clinton Public School District, Clinton MS

Mississippi College is an amazing place. I received my undergraduate degree in Elementary Education from MC. The professors opened my eyes to a whole new world of education and leadership. I am forever indebted to the staff for helping me become a life-long learner and an effective leader.

Jana Carter
Assistant Principal, Hinds County Public Schools

The Elementary Education program at MC prepared me to be an effective and compassionate educator in today's schools. The professors were fantastic and truly cared about me and my education. I have loved my educational experiences at and through MC – the practical field experiences, the classes, the conversations, and my peers. I would not be the educator I am without the great support I received while completing my degrees from MC.

Brittany Ricker
Assistant Principal, Eastside Elementary, Clinton MS

Montana State University

Bozeman, MT

SCORE CARD

Elementary Indicators of Quality

Rigorous admissions process:	A+
Learning how to teach reading:	B
Preparing to teach math:	B
High quality practice teaching:	D
Learning to manage the classroom:	B

Secondary Indicators of Quality

Rigorous admissions process:	A+
Content preparation (social studies, science):	A
High quality practice teaching:	D
Learning to manage the classroom:	B

Where do candidates student teach?

- Bozeman School District
- Livingston School District
- Belgrade School District

What's special

Dean's Statement – Elementary

One of the distinguishing characteristics of the Montana State University Teacher Education program is its commitment to field experience throughout the program. Students complete a service-learning experience as part of their educational psychology course (typically in the first or second year). This exposes students to the teaching profession before they are officially admitted into the Teacher Education Program and helps them to understand if teaching is the profession for them. This field experience is then complemented with an after school experience, in which students develop and teach lessons either as part of book club or tech club with elementary through middle school students. Finally, Department of Education coordinates Montana State University's America Reads / America Counts program which provides students, particularly those eligible to receive federal work study, the opportunity to enhance local K-12 students' literacy or math skills. These field experiences compliment the required field practicum and student teaching, enabling our students to develop a strong pedagogical and content foundation to begin as in-service teachers.

Where do graduates work?

Elementary

- Billings School District
- Great Falls School District
- Montforton School District

Secondary

- Bozeman School District
- Kalispell School District
- Bainville School District

Campus Facts at a Glance

Size:	Medium
Location:	Town
Acceptance rate:	83%
Student to faculty ratio:	19 to 1
Graduation rate:	51%
Is education a top 5 major:	No

Financial

In-state tuition:	$6,887
Out-of-state tuition:	$23,186
In-state average annual cost:	$16,809
Students receiving federal loans:	45%
Typical debt:	$24,000
Typical Montana new teacher salary:	**$27,274**

What's special about Montana State University

Dean's Statement – Secondary

A strength of the MSU secondary education program is our connection with high schools across the state of Montana. Montana State University requires all students to complete a university seminar course as part of the core curriculum. We offer the education-specific seminar course, EDU 101 Teaching & Enrollment, in 10 high schools as dual enrollment. This allows aspiring teacher education majors to complete college coursework while still in high school and at half the cost of standard on-campus university credits. In response to a growing teacher shortage in rural areas of Montana, the Department of Education has developed a teaching practicum field experience, allowing students to experience teaching and living in rural Montana as part of their coursework. Finally, MSU has partnered with the Montana Rural Education Association to offer Rural Teaching Fellows Scholarships, which provide financial support for teacher candidates to complete their student teaching in rural areas where a teaching need exists.

Candidates' Observations – Elementary

I would recommend the MSU Teacher Preparation Program to prospective students because of the outstanding faculty, exposure to the classroom, and opportunities to get involved in the community. As a student, I got to work with students right away in an after school book club program and as a CAP mentor volunteer at a school close to the University. The program's amazing advisors worked with me to make sure I was taking the necessary classes, and they made it possible for me to complete a practicum abroad in Toowoomba, Australia. I had the privilege of participating and organizing community events at the local schools with my professors and fellow classmates. Additionally, I was able to make positive, lasting connections with local teachers and administrators. I would highly recommend the MSU Teacher Preparation Program to interested students. This program gives people the skills needed to step into the classroom after graduation and be extraordinary teachers.

Stephanie White

Each professor at MSU has their own, distinct teaching style that exposes students to all types of educational methods and philosophies. This environment is highly conducive for pre-service teachers to develop their teaching practices according to their personal style.

Cassie McCann

Candidates' Observations – Secondary

Prospective teachers should consider the program at MSU because of the quality of the professors. The amount of in the classroom experience they bring with them is an invaluable resource to those of us who are just starting out. All the expertise an MSU student could ask for is readily available.

Wes Webb

The Montana State Teacher Education Program provides many options and resources that allow students to customize their degrees and learning experiences to align with their personal passions and interests. This gives students the opportunity to get as much out of their degree as possible, increasing the likelihood that graduates will obtain jobs in the profession. Consequently, I would absolutely recommend this program to people who are looking to become teachers.

Lauren Hausauer

MSU offers a rigor-based, responsible, and educational program that helps future educators focus on the important role that they play. If asked to, I would happily tell anyone who was curious about the field to seek out the awesome education staff at MSU.

Jakob Wilson

Northwest Nazarene University
Nampa, ID

SCORE CARD
Secondary Indicators of Quality

Rigorous admissions process:	**A**
Content preparation (social studies, science):	**A**
High quality practice teaching:	**C**
Learning to manage the classroom:	**B**

100% (2014–2015) **100%** (2015–2016)
GRADUATE AND GO RIGHT INTO TEACHING

What's special

Dean's Statement

Educators across the region view the Department of Education programs at Northwest Nazarene University as the best teacher preparation programs in the northwest. Because our graduates are highly sought after by principals seeking to hire the best-prepared teachers, our annual employment rate over the past five years is 100% among graduates seeking teaching jobs after receiving their education degree and certification.

The Education Department at Northwest Nazarene University recognizes its professional responsibility to ensure programs and graduates of the highest quality. We are committed to equipping schools with caring, competent professionals who have the knowledge, dispositions, and abilities to positively impact student learning and development.

Northwest Nazarene University teacher preparation programs are guided by our conceptual framework, the Learner-Centered CORE, which outlines the goals of the faculty to produce teachers who are called to serve, open to change, responsive to all, and empowered to succeed. We know teaching is not just a job; it is a profession of service to others and involves the transformation of lives. If you want to teach, and be the best at it, come to Northwest Nazarene University.

Where do candidates student teach?
- Nampa School District
- Caldwell School District
- Kuna School District

Where do graduates work?
- Nampa School District
- Caldwell School District
- Kuna School District

Campus Facts at a Glance

Size:	Small
Location:	Suburban
Acceptance rate:	95%
Student to faculty ratio:	15 to 1
Graduation rate:	51%
Is education a top 5 major:	Yes

Financial

Out-of-state tuition:	$28,650
In-state average annual cost:	$19,432
Students receiving federal loans:	62%
Typical debt:	$26,000

**Typical Idaho
new teacher salary:** $31,159

What's special about Northwest Nazarene University

Candidates' Observations

Trusting me as a responsible and independent student was the first thing that made me feel respected as a future teacher. The classes were not easy which would have been a huge red flag. I knew I had to work hard to be successful. Classes were diverse in their content and had a variety of professors with different backgrounds. There was flexibility during my student teaching that was a grand improvement and had a positive effect on my whole experience.

The program included a good variety of coursework and we learned through experience. I think the best thing NNU did was pair me with an excellent mentor teacher for student teaching. She continued to support me even after I graduated and really made me a good teacher. I also felt that NNU did us a service by providing numerous classroom experiences for all four years.

I am so much better prepared to teach, compared to the other new teachers in my building. The education department at NNU has the best reputation around for building excellent teachers. I had several schools who wanted to hire me as I was finishing my student teaching.

NNU's Program provided me with the opportunities to practice writing units which helped me develop organized curriculum with formative and summative assessments. I also continue to use my weekly and long term teaching schedules to plan and prepare my units.

I am confident in planning, preparation, and delivery of material and I can discuss frameworks now with a foundation of understanding in place. Very prepared. Thank you, NNU!

Purdue University
West Lafayette, IN

Outstanding Program

SCORE CARD

Elementary Indicators of Quality
Rigorous admissions process:	A+
Learning how to teach reading:	A
Preparing to teach math:	A
High quality practice teaching:	C
Learning to manage the classroom:	A

Secondary Indicators of Quality
Rigorous admissions process:	A+
Content preparation (social studies, science):	A
High quality practice teaching:	C
Learning to manage the classroom:	C

96% ELEMENTARY 97% SECONDARY
GRADUATE AND GO RIGHT INTO TEACHING

Where do candidates student teach?
Elementary
- Tippecanoe School Corporation
- Lafayette School Corporation
- West Lafayette Community School Corporation

Secondary
- Lafayette School Corporation
- Tippecanoe School Corporation
- Lafayette Catholic School System

Where do graduates work?
- Indianapolis Public Schools
- Lafayette School Corporation
- Tippecanoe School Corporation

Campus Facts at a Glance
Size:	Large
Location:	Suburban
Acceptance rate:	56%
Student to faculty ratio:	12 to 1
Graduation rate:	74%
Is education a top 5 major:	No

Financial
In-state tuition:	$10,002
Out-of-state tuition:	$28,804
In-state average annual cost:	$13,516
Students receiving federal loans:	33%
Typical debt:	$21,500

Typical Indiana new teacher salary: **$34,696**

What's special

Dean's Statement – Elementary

The teacher education program at Purdue offers the best of both worlds: a small and respected College of Education within a Big Ten research university. You will be part of a dynamic campus where scientific breakthroughs and the discovery of new knowledge changes lives while you are preparing to change the lives of the students you will teach. Our fully accredited elementary education program provides in-depth content knowledge, extensive methods training, and hours of clinical experience.

(continued on next page)

What's special about Purdue University

Dean's Statement – Elementary

You will be in actual classrooms with partner teachers throughout your entire program, beginning in your first year of study. Ours is a welcoming community that values diversity, equity and inclusion – and we encourage our students to do the same. Be prepared to make a difference. At Purdue's College of Education, we launch the future through the discovery and development of human potential.

Candidates' Observations – Elementary

The College of Education at Purdue University is one of the smallest colleges on campus. Because of this, we become family. I have had professors who treated me as their colleague instead of their student. The professors really get to know who you are. Dr. Bob as well as Dr. Kastberg took the time to include me in my education and that will stay with me forever. Over the past four years here, I became Gianna Mesarina, not student ID number XXXX. I would most definitely recommend this program to others. Purdue's motto states, "We make what moves the world forward" and with that mentality in mind, we truly are getting the skills and concepts to be able to move the world forward one day.

Gianna V. Mesarina, *Elementary Education*

The teacher education program at Purdue goes above and beyond in preparing exceptional educators for the professional world. The research opportunities at this institute go above and beyond what anyone could expect, especially when you are given the privilege of working under the tutelage of world-renowned researchers and professors. The rigorous and effective program challenges you and brings out your best potential, allowing you to grow and expand your horizons as a global citizen. I would highly recommend this program to anyone interested in anything related to education, such as becoming a teacher or education researcher. The early field experiences, small class sizes, world class professors, and endless professional development and research opportunities are just a few ways Purdue's teacher education program is outstanding.

Monerah N. Al-Dubayan, *Special/Elementary Education*

What makes Purdue's College of Education special is the commitment of the faculty and staff to making learning meaningful and preparing students to become teachers. All of my professors have been eager to get to know students and help them become the best version of themselves. The College of Education is also great because it gets future teachers into classrooms right away. I was a secondary education major upon starting at Purdue, and my first semester I was in a high school classroom. The staff in the advising office helped me get into an elementary classroom that same semester when I was unsure if high school was for me. Because of the College of Education's commitment to the students, I was able to switch majors and find that my passion lies in working with younger kids. I would recommend this program to anyone interested in education because of the connections the faculty makes with students, the willingness of the staff to help students succeed and become great teachers, and the experiences offered through the College of Education, like practicums, study abroad programs, leadership opportunities, and student organizations.

TJ Rosa, *Elementary Education*

Candidates' Observations – Secondary

Agricultural Education at Purdue has some great opportunities! The first is our 3-week agriculture education study abroad to Jamaica. There you take classes with our professors and visit many farms and schools. It was my first time leaving the country but I had so much fun and learned a lot, too! We also have an agriculture education internship where you are placed with an FFA Chapter over the summer and are paid to help with SAE Visits, State FFA Convention, summer trips, county fair, and other events that the agriculture teacher helps with over the summer. It is a great opportunity to see what it is like to be an agriculture teacher outside of the classroom. I was unsure if I wanted to teach before doing the internship, but during my internship, I realized that teaching is definitely where I belong. Another great thing about Purdue Agriculture Education is that you have many agriculture selective classes. We can use these either to specialize in a specific area of agriculture or to get a broad understanding of agriculture. I am double minoring in crop science and horticulture and still graduating on time!

Elizabeth Brown, *Agriculture Education*

University of Alaska Fairbanks
Fairbanks, AK

SCORE CARD

Elementary Indicators of Quality

Rigorous admissions process:	**A+**
Learning how to teach reading:	**A**
Preparing to teach math:	**D**
High quality practice teaching:	**A**
Learning to manage the classroom:	**A**

93% (2014-2015) **93%** (2015-2016)
GRADUATE AND GO RIGHT INTO TEACHING

Where do graduates work?
- Fairbanks North Star Borough School District
- Matanuska-Susitna School District and Anchorage School District
- Lower Kuskokwim School District

What's special

Dean's Statement

For decades, the UAF Bachelor of Arts in Elementary Education Program has successfully prepared its students for the challenges of teaching in Alaska's elementary classrooms. Evidence of this success is that each year school districts across Alaska recruit our students. Our Elementary Program offers a personal experience with students regularly meeting with faculty and advisors. We maintain excellent relationships with all of Alaska's K-12 communities and provide students opportunities for their internship anywhere in the state. This yearlong internship is an intensive experience where students apply the theory of practice with observing master teachers and teaching elementary students.

(continued on next page)

Where do candidates student teach?
- Fairbanks North Star Borough School District
- Matanuska-Susitna School District and Anchorage School District
- Lower Kuskokwim School District

Campus Facts at a Glance

Size:	Medium
Location:	Suburban
Acceptance rate:	73%
Student to faculty ratio:	9 to 1
Graduation rate:	30%
Is education a top 5 major:	No

Financial

In-state tuition:	$5,976
Out-of-state tuition:	$18,184
In-state average annual cost:	$9,942
Students receiving federal loans:	25%
Typical debt:	$16,976

Typical Alaska new teacher salary:	**$44,166**

What's special about University of Alaska Fairbanks

Dean's Statement

The UAF Bachelors of Elementary Education Program is based on core practices that include an emphasis on place-based education. This and other foundational pieces of the program well prepare our graduates to work in a remote Alaskan village or in a traditional urban elementary school. We regularly improve our program by analyzing feedback from our students and graduates, staying current with research, and maintaining close ties with K-12 and state initiatives to then refine our courses and program design. The quality of our program, excellent job placement and UAF's competitive tuition make the UAF SOE BA in Elementary Education a degree worth pursuing.

Candidates' Observations

I would recommend this program to students who are looking to become teachers because it is a program with a wonderful support system. While the work is rigorous and at times challenging, it is for the better. The faculty at the University of Alaska, Fairbanks School of Elementary Education truly cares about their students. They want what is best for their students and will support them in their endeavors.

I have a great deal of confidence in the program for turning out young and talented teachers. They not only teach students to strive for excellence, but they teach them the tools to connect with students and be the teacher that changes a students' life.

I cannot thank the School of Education at UAF enough for what they have done for me. I loved it so much that I am continuing on in school for my Master's Degree in Special Education through the UAF Elementary Education Program.

If you're looking for an exceptional program to help refine your skills in teaching, this is the one!

Emma Henze-Nelson

I would highly recommend UAF because of the following reasons:

- The instructors and staff are supportive, understanding, and have a vast knowledge and a wide range of experiences specific to elementary classrooms
- The year-long internship provides a start-to-finish in-the-trenches experience of what being an elementary teacher is like
- All of the course work up to and including the courses during the internship year prepare pre-service teachers to teach in Fairbanks with resources to teach in Alaska as a whole
- Mentor teachers and university liaisons are present for the entire internship year to guide and support pre-service teachers as we teach in a classroom

Natasha Farley McCleery

The education program at UAF provides dynamic preparation for teaching. From my very first semester of college, they provided opportunities for me to be involved in local classrooms and schools. The School of Education made it a point to match students with successful and innovative teachers around the community.

By far the most powerful learning came through the year-long internship program required for the degree! This program allowed for practical learning. From working with colleagues, communicating with parents, designing lessons, and honing classroom management, the SOE provided many opportunities to develop us as teachers. Their work has proven successful as I was able to get a job right away! Though I still have a lot to learn as a new teacher, I feel prepared for my first year thanks to the education I received from UAF.

Miranda Thiessen

- The UAF Elementary Ed program is so well rounded that I never felt that I was missing out or not receiving the education needed to become the best teacher.
- The hours spent in the classroom and the practicum work prepared me for the realities of what can and might happen in the classroom as an intern and as a teacher.
- UAF's education program teachers and staff are so personable and so knowledgeable that many of the things we learn about in our text books are applicable and are talked about during the stories the teachers share of their own experiences
- The class sizes at UAF are small enough that you are an actual person in the classroom and the teachers really care about your learning.
- The cohort you begin with during your freshman or sophomore year has the same classmates you'll have your senior year so you have such a relationship with your classmates and you can always count on them!

Charity Moore

What's special about University of Alaska Fairbanks

Candidates' Observations

- The UAF School of Education BAE program is full of faculty that are there to guide and support future teachers. The faculty cares about their students and offers their knowledge and experiences to advise future educators.

- Alaska is strong in its cultural values and the UAF School of Education BAE program holds those values close in the choice of their instructors, courses, and lessons.

Cassie Kendall

1. The UAF BA Elementary Education program provides aspiring teachers with hands on opportunities in a variety of classrooms. Being able to participate and see multiple teaching strategies helped prepare me for my future classroom.

2. The professors in this program are invested in making sure you become successful and are willing to go out of their way to make it happen.

Caitlin Brice

I'd recommend the UAF School of Education as the program for future teachers because of the enriched experience it provides. Not only do you get the ability to start and finish a whole year with a class, but you are provided with the included opportunity to travel to rural Alaska to experience the way culture can impact learning in our great state. The program has also provided me with tools to help me as a teacher who is dedicated to consistently assessing my students for progress through using the Literacy Development Profile. My year in the Student-Teacher Intern Program at UAF was a challenging yet extremely rewarding experience.

Ashley Pruitt

Our program is rooted in the schools and connects you to skilled teachers, some of the best I've ever met.

Much of what you learn you get to apply in your fieldwork, making it more practical in nature.

Many of the classes' books are lesson-planning guides, which are affordable and very useful through the program and after graduation.

Sam Schmidt

University of Houston
Houston, TX

SCORE CARD
Elementary Indicators of Quality

Rigorous admissions process:	**A+**
Learning how to teach reading:	**A**
Preparing to teach math:	**F**
High quality practice teaching:	**A**
Learning to manage the classroom:	**A**

81%* OR 89%** (2014-2015) **72%** (2015-2016)
GRADUATE AND GO RIGHT INTO TEACHING

Where do graduates work?
- Houston Independent School District
- Cypress-Fairbanks Independent School District
- Alief Independent School District

What's special

Dean's Statement

The University of Houston College of Education strives to prepare teachers who are classroom ready on day one. Our students gain valuable real-world experience through a yearlong student-teaching internship and receive on-site coaching from our instructors and mentor teachers.

We also work to help students receive financial aid and scholarships. For example, the University of Houston was selected in 2017 to be part of the Raising Texas Teachers initiative, which increases our capacity to provide financial support to teaching majors.

(continued on next page)

Where do candidates student teach?
- Houston Independent School District
- Fort Bend Independent School District
- Cypress-Fairbanks Independent School District

Campus Facts at a Glance

Size:	Medium
Location:	City
Acceptance rate:	59%
Student to faculty ratio:	21 to 1
Graduation rate:	16
Is education a top 5 major:	No

Financial

In-state tuition:	$9,519
Out-of-state tuition:	$21,711
In-state average annual cost:	$7,465
Students receiving federal loans:	43%
Typical debt:	$18,750
Typical Texas new teacher salary:	**$38,091**

* Rate includes teaching majors with an elementary education specialization who were employed in Texas public schools. Does not include those employed by private schools or out of state and does not include those whose names have changed since graduation.

** 89% is the employment rate published by the Texas Higher Education Coordinating Board. It includes all teaching majors who were employed in jobs in Texas or nationally, based on data from the Texas Workforce Commission and the U.S. Office of Personnel. Data for 2015-16 is not available from the Coordinating Board.

What's special about University of Houston

Dean's Statement – Elementary

In addition, we partner with dozens of school districts in the Houston area, so we understand their needs and ensure our graduates are prepared to teach in diverse contexts. Graduates of our program are more likely to retain their positions than those who did alternative certification. We believe in high standards. Our teacher-prep program was the first in Texas to be accredited under the new, tougher criteria set by the Council for the Accreditation of Educator Preparation.

The college is a proud member of the national reform network US PREP, allowing us to collaborate with other colleges to continue to transform teacher preparation. We are committed to eliminating disparities in education so the next generation of leaders and innovators can thrive.

Dean Robert McPherson, *Ph.D., University of Houston College of Education*

Candidates' Observations

The methods classes have really helped me understand the art of teaching. I wouldn't change the University of Houston for anything. I most definitely feel like I'm going to be prepared. With my Student Teaching I experience, if I had a question, my cooperating teacher would reply to me within an hour or so. I've had great instructors and cooperating teachers.

Cecilia Cardona, *senior*

I really love it. Even though we are in college, we learn by doing. For example, in my math class, we had manipulatives, and the professor was teaching us with manipulatives how we should teach our kids in the classroom. Not only that, but we were asked to come up with new ideas and strategies to help the kids learn.

Laura Respondek, *senior*

The yearlong student teaching experience through UH sealed the deal for me wanting to be a teacher. I did my internship at Tanglewood Middle School as a science teacher. About half the students at the school were low income, and many were English Language Learners like I was. It was great being able to see the school year from beginning to end. We started the year planting a garden, teaching the students about ecosystems and sustainability. It was great being able to work with other teachers on a huge cross-curricular project that taught students how to apply what they were learning in the classroom to a real problem-solving situation.

Aljay Tan, *May 2017 graduate*

The yearlong internship was key. I've talked to friends who went to other colleges and only student taught for one semester. They feel far less prepared to start teaching on day one.

Lauren DeVault, *May 2017 graduate*

University of Iowa
Iowa City, IA

SCORE CARD

Elementary Indicators of Quality

Rigorous admissions process:	A
Learning how to teach reading:	D
Preparing to teach math:	A
High quality practice teaching:	A
Learning to manage the classroom:	A

Secondary Indicators of Quality

Rigorous admissions process:	A
Content preparation (social studies, science):	A/C
High quality practice teaching:	A
Learning to manage the classroom:	A

74% (2014-2015) 78% (2015-2016)
GRADUATE AND GO RIGHT INTO TEACHING

Where do graduates work?
- Iowa City Community School District
- Cedar Rapids Community School District
- West Liberty Community School District

What's special

Dean's Statement – Elementary

The Teacher Education Program at the University of Iowa is the state of Iowa's only program to offer a professional development series that integrates technology, assessment, and school community training into a Teacher Leader Certificate. This certificate, as well as the one-to-one technology platforms and devices provided by the College, help our teacher leaders stay at the forefront of educational technologies related to student learning and engagement. The University of Iowa's College of Education and Teacher Education Program is Iowa's highest ranked education program, with a teacher retention rate of more than 85% continuing to work in education 5 years after graduation.

Daniel Clay
Dean, The University of Iowa College of Education

Where do candidates student teach?
- Iowa City Community School District
- Clear Creek Amana Community School District
- Cedar Rapids Community School District

Campus Facts at a Glance

Size:	Large
Location:	City
Acceptance rate:	84%
Student to faculty ratio:	15 to 1
Graduation rate:	71%
Is education a top 5 major:	No

Financial

In-state tuition:	$8,575
Out-of-state tuition:	$28,813
In-state average annual cost:	$14,085
Students receiving federal loans:	44%
Typical debt:	$21,616

Typical Iowa new teacher salary: **$33,226**

What's special about University of Iowa

Candidates' Observations – Elementary

The Teacher Education Program at the University of Iowa is special because of our great professors who really know how to prepare us for our future career. An example of an excellent professor is Renita Schmidt. Before taking her class I was hesitant about teaching children how to read, but after only a semester with her I felt confident about my skills in teaching both advanced and struggling readers. Our program is also great because of our small class sizes, and the amount of time we get to spend in the classroom before starting our student teaching experience. It really is a close knit community that becomes a family on a college campus.

Brittany Struve
Elementary Education, University of Iowa

I have known since I was a little kid that I wanted to be a teacher, and my time in the University of Iowa Teacher Education Program has reassured me of that. This program revolves around making us feel comfortable as future educators, and also allows us to try new things. We are able to figure out the kind of teacher each of us wants to individually be. This feeling of knowing who I am and the type of teacher I want to be is made possible by the amazing teachers I have had the opportunity to learn from in the program. Specifically, professors Robert Van Deusen, Renita Schmidt, and Brian Lehman have been three of the most influential educators and role models to me. They have provided me with knowledge and resources to take with me into the teaching world, but more importantly they have pushed me out of my comfort zone and encouraged me to try new things as I take on the role of a teacher. I feel so grateful and honored to be a part of the University of Iowa Teacher Education Program and proud to be a future hawkeye teacher!

Kelsey Schonhoff
Elementary Education, University of Iowa

Candidates' Observations – Secondary

I would recommend Iowa's Teacher Education Program because the professors genuinely care about your success in and out of the classroom. They not only want to help prepare you to be the best possible teacher, but also want to see you succeed in all areas of your life. In addition, the resources and opportunities provided through the Teacher Education Program, as well as the material covered in the classes, have helped me grow tremendously as a pre-service teacher and have prepared me for when I have a classroom of my own.

Matthew Hoffmann
Secondary Education – Social Studies, University of Iowa

University of Maryland – College Park
College Park, MD

SCORE CARD
Elementary Indicators of Quality

Rigorous admissions process:	**A+**
Learning how to teach reading:	**A**
Preparing to teach math:	**A**
High quality practice teaching:	**D**
Learning to manage the classroom:	**C**

93% (2014-2015) **94%** (2015-2016)
GRADUATE AND GO RIGHT INTO TEACHING

What's special

Dean's Statement

The University of Maryland College of Education's undergraduate elementary program provides innovative content and extensive field experience. As the College's most highly-enrolled teacher preparation program, its cutting-edge academics and hands-on learning opportunities appeal to a wide range of students.

The College Park campus, located near Washington, D.C., allows elementary education students access to a broad variety of schools – urban and suburban – for field placements. Our partner schools serve diverse populations, providing a context for teacher candidates to adapt instruction to meet the academic needs of all students.

Program courses emphasize pedagogy for effectively teaching students with disabilities, language variations, and multilingual backgrounds. Through coursework that features model instructional practices, such as arts integration and technology applications, our graduates are equipped to innovate in the classroom.

Our teacher candidates complete rigorous performance assessments aligned to the State's teacher evaluation system and conduct research-based projects that document their impact on student learning.

(continued on next page)

Where do candidates student teach?
- Montgomery County Public Schools
- Prince George's County Public Schools
- Anne Arundel County Public Schools

Where do graduates work?
- Montgomery County Public Schools
- Prince George's County Public Schools
- Anne Arundel County Public Schools

Campus Facts at a Glance

Size:	Large
Location:	Suburban
Acceptance rate:	48%
Student to faculty ratio:	17 to 1
Graduation rate:	86%
Is education a top 5 major:	No

Financial

In-state tuition:	$10,181
Out-of-state tuition:	$32,045
In-state average annual cost:	$15,634
Students receiving federal loans:	34%
Typical debt:	$19,500

Typical Maryland new teacher salary:	**$43,235**

What's special about University of Maryland – College Park

Dean's Statement

Teacher candidates spend four semesters in the field. As in medicine, they become "residents" in their field placement schools. They receive job-embedded professional development through classroom "rounds." Residents and faculty form professional learning communities where teaching is observed, reflected upon, and adapted based on discussion and research-based practice.

Candidates' Observations

I always felt supported by my teachers and advisor. I think the faculty is a big strength. Maggie Peterson, Lisa Bote and John O'Flahavan were the teacher's whose instruction stuck with me the most. Each of them was so passionate about their job and were so excited to share their experiences and guide us through our journey.

Comprehensive curriculum thoroughly covered all aspects of elementary education, multiple opportunities to apply practice in school environment, consistent support from advisors and professors. This program has fully prepared me for my future classroom.

A lot of exposure to kids. I had 4 different field placements where I got to learn from other teachers in our partner schools. Also, our professors teach us about the population we will be working with. I learned a lot about ELL students, and then worked in schools with many ELL students.

I was happy to be a part of the new program. Although there were a few bumps in the road, I found it to be a very beneficial change. I liked that we were able to have a junior placement because I think that made the transition into senior year much smoother. I also liked being there in January because I think the transition into takeover was smoother if less time was missed. The courses also provided important instruction in the arts, disabilities, and technology, which are all growing aspects of the field. I was also thankful to have such strong support from the coordinators and professors in the program and felt that most of them were there to help me learn and grow.

Our program was full of a variety of experiences inside the classroom. This was the best way to learn and it was so wonderful to experience a multitude of grades, counties, mentors, and schools.

University of Mississippi
University, MS

SCORE CARD

Elementary Indicators of Quality	
Rigorous admissions process:	A
Learning how to teach reading:	A
Preparing to teach math:	A
High quality practice teaching:	C
Learning to manage the classroom:	C

Secondary Indicators of Quality	
Rigorous admissions process:	A
Content preparation (social studies, science):	A
High quality practice teaching:	C
Learning to manage the classroom:	C

64% (2014-2015) **53%** (2015-2016) IN ELEMENTARY
45% (2014-2015) **57%** (2015-2016) IN SECONDARY
GRADUATE AND GO RIGHT INTO TEACHING

Where do graduates work?
- DeSoto County School District
- Tupelo Public School District
- Lee County School District

Where do candidates student teach?
Elementary
- DeSoto County School District
- Oxford School District
- Tupelo Public School District

Secondary
- Lafayette County School District
- Oxford School District
- Tupelo Public School District

Campus Facts at a Glance
Size:	Large
Location:	Town
Acceptance rate:	78%
Student to faculty ratio:	18 to 1
Graduation rate:	61%
Is education a top 5 major:	Yes

Financial
In-state tuition:	$7,744
Out-of-state tuition:	$22,012
In-state average annual cost:	$14,284
Students receiving federal loans:	44%
Typical debt:	$20,000

Typical Mississippi new teacher salary:	**$31,184**

What's special

Dean's Statement

Each day in communities across the nation, members of the School of Education (SOE) family at the University of Mississippi (UM) make the world a better place by providing exceptional teaching, leadership and service in schools and communities. Our students learn by doing through meaningful, hands-on experiences inside and outside the classroom by working with a variety of partners to improve learning for all children.

(continued on next page)

What's special about University of Mississippi

Dean's Statement

You can become part of the Mississippi Excellence in Teaching Program (METP), one of the top scholarships in the nation for top performing high school students who want to become outstanding educators. In 2017, 13 graduating SOE seniors earned UM's highest academic honor – the Taylor Medal. Not only do each of these students bring honor to themselves, but to the education profession as well. These graduates were selected as being among the top one percent of the university's graduating class at the university. Taylor Medalists do not merely have near-perfect GPAs, they must demonstrate how they have made a real and positive change in the world around them. This type of recognition demonstrates that students in the School of Education are not only passionate, dedicated, future educators but also some of the best students at the university.

Candidates' Observations

I feel very prepared to be an effective teacher! As an education student, I felt empathy and respect from my professors that I will definitely practice for the rest of my life. Also, allowing students to learn from their mistakes and have real life experiences was a very important part of my education.

Leticia Ruiz, B.A.Ed., 2017

The Ole Miss Teacher Education Program prepared me to be an effective teacher through several avenues. The coursework rigor, faculty knowledge and support, and student teaching experience were a three-fold collaboration which allowed me to secure a teaching position and to start teaching with confidence on day one.

University of Oklahoma
Norman, OK

SCORE CARD
Elementary Indicators of Quality

Rigorous admissions process:	A+
Learning how to teach reading:	B
Preparing to teach math:	A
High quality practice teaching:	D
Learning to manage the classroom:	F

What's special

Dean's Statement

The University of Oklahoma College of Education's nationally recognized Elementary Education program is truly a hands-on experience for students. As soon as students are admitted to the elementary education major, they begin targeted experiences in classrooms. Undergraduate students complete field experiences in rural, urban and suburban settings in a variety of local schools observing and tutoring children in basic skills. This real-world education is coupled with classes that emphasize deep subject area content and research-based curriculum on learning and motivation and classroom management. The program of study focuses on first grade through sixth grade (and possibly up to eighth grade) in social studies, science, language arts and math. Students also study educational psychology, child development, pedagogy and teaching methodology. The program culminates in intensive mentored teaching opportunities in the pre-internship practicum and the student teaching internship, assuring that graduates are well-prepared to be a positive influence in the lives of children from day one in their own classrooms.

Where do candidates student teach?
- Norman Public Schools
- Moore Public Schools
- Noble Public Schools

Where do graduates work?
- Norman Public Schools
- Moore Public Schools
- Yukon Public Schools

Campus Facts at a Glance

Size:	Large
Location:	Suburban
Acceptance rate:	71%
Student to faculty ratio:	18 to 1
Graduation rate:	67%
Is education a top 5 major:	No

Financial

In-state tuition:	$10,881
Out-of-state tuition:	$25,203
In-state average annual cost:	$16,418
Students receiving federal loans:	35%
Typical debt:	$20,000

Typical Oklahoma new teacher salary:	**$31,606**

What's special about University of Oklahoma

Candidates' Observations

I think the college did a great job of training me for a technology-driven classroom. I am very aware of how to use my iPad for teaching; I have been exposed to apps that are great for reading, math and STEM; and I feel like I am able to help my students use their technology in a meaningful way.

Morgan Dunnagan

What I most appreciate about my time with the Jeannine Rainbolt College of Education is the guidance, support and room I was given to navigate multiple learning and teaching styles in order to develop my unique brand as an educator.

Josh Flores

Dean Garn and the many educators I came across during my time in the Jeannine Rainbolt College of Education showed me the value in genuinely investing my time, love and support into the lives of my future students. By implementing the concepts and practices I learned while at OU, I was able to successfully transition into the workplace and even be recognized as the Norman Public Schools Rookie Teacher of the Year.

Juanito Renteria

University of South Carolina – Columbia
Columbia, SC

SCORE CARD
Elementary Indicators of Quality
Rigorous admissions process:	**A**
Learning how to teach reading:	**F**
Preparing to teach math:	**A**
High quality practice teaching:	**D**
Learning to manage the classroom:	**B**

What's special

Dean's Statement

What sets apart the Elementary Education program at the University of South Carolina is the integrative field experiences that begin when candidates arrive on campus and continue throughout the program. Too often teacher education programs privilege theory and expect candidates to imagine what it means for classroom practice. Our program is well known and respected for its innovative courses because they are designed to offer intentional and systematic opportunities for candidates to theorize from practice each and every class period. This unique school – university collaboration requires participants to position themselves as learners in ways that promote the professional development of teachers, candidates and university faculty, and ultimately student growth. In short, the courses are designed to promote professional inquiry while simultaneously fostering content inquiry with elementary students.

By engaging in carefully crafted experiences, candidates learn to make meaning of theories originating in classroom practice and develop theories of their own. In this way, teacher candidates construct practical knowledge alongside theoretical concepts. By teaching courses onsite in elementary schools and collaboratively planning embedded field experiences with exemplary classroom teachers, candidates are offered the chance to witness, reflect upon and implement exemplary teaching demonstrations that are directly related to the beliefs and practices they are learning in their courses.

Where do candidates student teach?
- Richland County School District 1
- Richland School District 2
- Lexington-Richland School District 5

Where do graduates work?
- Richland School District 2
- Richland County School District 1
- Lexington County School District 1

Campus Facts at a Glance
Size:	Large
Location:	City
Acceptance rate:	68%
Student to faculty ratio:	18 to 1
Graduation rate:	73%
Is education a top 5 major:	No

Financial
In-state tuition:	$11,454
Out-of-state tuition:	$30,882
In-state average annual cost:	$18,555
Students receiving federal loans:	48%
Typical debt:	$23,250

Typical South Carolina new teacher salary: **$32,306**

What's special about University of South Carolina – Columbia

Candidates' Observations

This program can get you into the classroom as soon as your freshman year. This early access was beneficial as it confirmed I was right where I wanted to be. Leaving that first day observing in a classroom I was ecstatic that what I had known I wanted to do since fifth grade was finally beginning, and I looked forward to continuing. For some of my education peers it was beneficial as well, as it led them to seek a different direction. Getting into the classroom so soon allowed everyone in the program to make a decision about their college path. From someone who looked at other programs before deciding on USC's, I have never seen a program that gets their potential teachers in the classroom so soon. From my experience already and going into my last year, I have gained knowledge and skills to prepare me to start my teaching career, and it's all thanks to the elementary education program at The University of South Carolina.

Abby Fraser

I would recommend this program to anyone who wants to be fully supported and immersed in learning to teach. This program is one with some of the most caring and intelligent professors who want only to see you succeed in becoming a teacher for the future. This program cares not only about their students, but the children that they interact with. The University of South Carolina takes their dispositions seriously and holds their students to the highest level of expectations. I would choose this school over any other because I know that no matter the time in my career, I will have these people, these memories, and this support for the rest of my life. When you choose to be an educator, you take on the role of being a leader, a learner forever, a guardian, and an open pair of arms. But when you choose to be an educator from the University of South Carolina, you choose to be the best you can be, because the best there has taught you how.

Madeline Donaway

The USC College of Education is such an exemplary program because it provides immediate classroom immersion and a personable, knowledgeable faculty. I had the opportunity to observe in a classroom my freshman year as an Elementary Education major. There is such a vast number of pre-service teaching experiences in real classrooms which have given me the tools to begin to develop my own teaching methods and grow as a future educator. In addition to the prompt and frequent observational and teaching experiences, the College of Education faculty are incredibly passionate and knowledgeable about current teaching practices, subject content, and how to most effectively scaffold us to become teachers. The professors you will encounter in this program genuinely care about you and want you to succeed. These professors will become your greatest mentors, as they have for me. For example, I have had a science methods professor go above and beyond to help me gather and prepare materials for a complicated, hands-on experiment, and I have had a literacy methods professor model a reading conference with a student in front of our class to allow us to learn from a real demonstration. The faculty's dedication to providing the most authentic teaching preparation and experiences is one of many factors as to why this program is best-equipped to grow you in the role of a knowledgeable, responsive practitioner. Not only do these faculty members work to collaborate with local schools to provide immediate immersion in a real classroom setting, but the USC College of Education keeps us in the classroom, as our methods classes are also taught onsite at elementary schools to provide us with authentic transactions with the content and methods we are learning.

I would also recommend this program because it has given me experiences in diverse schools and classrooms, which will help prepare me for the future and teaching to a diverse group of learners. I have observed and taught lessons in schools of both high- and low-income areas, ESOL and Montessori classrooms, and a wide variety of grade levels, spanning the range for Elementary Education. Overall, this program has given me the resources, knowledge, confidence, and drive to become the best teacher I can and constantly grow as a reflective practitioner.

Emily Odom

University of Texas at Arlington
Arlington, TX

SCORE CARD

Elementary Indicators of Quality

Rigorous admissions process:	**A+**
Learning how to teach reading:	**A+**
Preparing to teach math:	**D**
High quality practice teaching:	**C**
Learning to manage the classroom:	**A**

78% (2014-2015) 81%* (2015-2016)
GRADUATE AND GO RIGHT INTO TEACHING

Where do graduates work?
- Arlington Independent School District
- Grand Prairie Independent School District
- Hurst-Euless-Bedford Independent School District

What's special

Dean's Statement

The Elementary program at the University of Texas at Arlington (UTA) is nationally accredited and offers high-quality educator preparation at an affordable cost. Located in the heart of the Dallas/Fort Worth Metroplex, our candidates engage in field experiences early in their program in a range of diverse elementary classrooms. They are able to apply the knowledge and skills they learn at UTA to real settings and students throughout their training. Our distinguished faculty prepare graduates to deliver high-quality educational services by providing rigorous programs and incorporating new knowledge generated through their impactful research.

(continued on next page)

Where do candidates student teach?
- Arlington Independent School District
- Grand Prairie Independent School District
- Mansfield Independent School District

Campus Facts at a Glance

Size:	Large
Location:	City
Acceptance rate:	70%
Student to faculty ratio:	25 to 1
Graduation rate:	44%
Is education a top 5 major:	No

Financial

In-state tuition:	$9,616
Out-of-state tuition:	$22,920
In-state average annual cost:	$14,059
Students receiving federal loans:	46%
Typical debt:	$18,000
Typical Texas new teacher salary:	**$38,091**

* For 2014-15, 78% of students took a teaching job in a Texas public or charter school after graduation. For 2015-16, the percentage was 81%. These percentages do not reflect those students that were hired by private schools and out-of-state schools. From our own College of Education biannual exit survey of undergraduate students, we have determined that 100% of those students who sought teaching positions were hired into teaching positions.

What's special about University of Texas at Arlington

Dean's Statement

Teacher education candidates in the College of Education have an opportunity to participate in student organizations and develop their leadership skills through the student ambassador program, Bilingual Education Student Organization, and Kappa Delta Pi. They are also a part of a vibrant and diverse urban campus community. We also offer high performing high school juniors and seniors an opportunity to enter into our UTA Teacher Academy where they may earn up to 24-hours of dual credit towards a bachelor's degree and thus, decrease their costs and time to degree. Our graduates make a difference in communities and in the lives of the children they teach.

Candidates' Observations

I would recommend this program to other people looking to become teachers because of the vast range of real-world experience my professors have. The professors have so much hands-on knowledge and incorporate that into their lectures. The experience they bring to share with us is priceless.

Melissa Garcia

I would strongly recommend this program to those who are considering becoming a teacher because of the hands-on training we get with children of all ages and the tremendous support of the professors from this program. They really help work with you to understand various concepts of teaching and how to apply them to the classroom.

Yasmin Mughal

I would recommend this program because it allows you to engage with the children and learn from teachers that have been teaching for a while. These teachers are great because they pass on their wisdom to future teachers. This allows us to see what they know and most of the time, what they are telling us is the same thing we are learning from the teachers in the schools.

Karley Rowe

University of Texas at Austin
Austin, TX

SCORE CARD
Elementary Indicators of Quality

Rigorous admissions process:	**A+**
Learning how to teach reading:	**F**
Preparing to teach math:	**A**
High quality practice teaching:	**C**
Learning to manage the classroom:	**A**

88% (2014-2015) **95%** (2015-2016)
GRADUATE AND GO RIGHT INTO TEACHING

What's special

Dean's Statement

The teacher preparation program at the College of Education at the University of Texas at Austin gives pre-service teachers the educational foundation, tools, and experiences they need to be successful educators of all the children they will meet in their classrooms. Our focus is on preparing teachers to provide culturally relevant education to students of all abilities and backgrounds. Our program goes above and beyond the state requirements, by providing students with over 800 hours of time in real classrooms during their field experiences and student teaching, where they not only interact with young students before they graduate, but are also guided and mentored by exceptional teachers. Because of the quality of the research-in-practice preparation they receive in our program, 90 percent of our teacher preparation program graduates are immediately employed.

Dr. Beth Maloch
Associate Dean of Teacher Education

Where do candidates student teach?
- Austin ISD
- Round Rock ISD
- Pflugerville ISD

Where do graduates work?
- Austin ISD
- Houston ISD
- Round Rock ISD

Campus Facts at a Glance

Size:	Large
Location:	City
Acceptance rate:	40%
Student to faculty ratio:	18 to 1
Graduation rate:	80%
Is education a top 5 major:	No

Financial

In-state tuition:	$10,092
Out-of-state tuition:	$35,682
In-state average annual cost:	$17,742
Students receiving federal loans:	36%
Typical debt:	$22,250

**Typical Texas
new teacher salary:** **$38,091**

What's special about University of Texas at Austin

Candidates' Observations

My reason for recommending this program is the College of Education's commitment to changing the future of education. I've seen how dedicated the coordinators and professors are to social justice and changing what education should look like in the classroom. This includes celebrating differences, while still building a sense of community in the classroom. I've also learned strategies to make math and science come to life for students so that learning is always authentic and student-centered. These days I think it's especially important that we study new ways to promote critical thinking and responsible, productive citizens.

Clemente Garcia

At UT, our professors instill in us a passion to learn, to care for our students, and to do what we can to change the course of education in the United States for the better. For anyone interested in making a difference in education, UT is the place to be!

Gabriela Coelho

I am leaving the teacher education program at UT feeling prepared and confident in my teaching abilities. I have gained such an amazing support system from the College of Education. We have the opportunity to work in a variety of placements and take a wide range of informative classes. This gives us more tools and experiences to become incredible teachers.

Amanda Parra

University of Utah
Salt Lake City, UT

SCORE CARD

Elementary Indicators of Quality

Rigorous admissions process:	A+
Learning how to teach reading:	A
Preparing to teach math:	A
High quality practice teaching:	D
Learning to manage the classroom:	B

Secondary Indicators of Quality

Rigorous admissions process:	A+
Content preparation (social studies, science):	A
High quality practice teaching:	A
Learning to manage the classroom:	B

85% (2014-2015) **85%** (2015-2016) IN ELEMENTARY
99% (2014-2015) **99%** (2015-2016) IN SECONDARY
GRADUATE AND GO RIGHT INTO TEACHING

Where do graduates work?

Elementary
- Granite School District
- Canyons School District
- Salt Lake City School District

Secondary
- Granite School District
- Charter Schools
- Salt Lake City School District

Where do candidates student teach?

Elementary
- Granite School District
- Salt Lake City School District

Secondary
- Granite School District
- Salt Lake City School District
- Murray School District

Campus Facts at a Glance

Size:	Large
Location:	City
Acceptance rate:	76%
Student to faculty ratio:	16 to 1
Graduation rate:	63%
Is education a top 5 major:	No

Financial

In-state tuition:	$8,518
Out-of-state tuition:	$27,039
In-state average annual cost:	$13,696
Students receiving federal loans:	34%
Typical debt:	$15,000
Typical Utah new teacher salary:	**$33,081**

What's special

Dean's Statement

Teacher education at the University of Utah is dedicated to the preparation of educators equipped with the knowledge, skills, and classroom-based experiences necessary for work in 21st century classrooms and schools. Elementary Education graduates are professionals committed, in word and action, to quality education for all children. Our graduates are *Student-Ready and Profession-Ready – Day One!*

(continued on next page)

What's special about University of Utah

Dean's Statement

The Elementary degree and licensure program at the University of Utah offers courses and classroom-based experiences informed by research and data on best practices for work in today's classrooms and schools. Our program emphases specifically address preparation for work with students from diverse backgrounds, life experiences, and abilities. Course work includes technology innovations, student diversity, literacy, science, and numeracy preparation, and knowledge of data-based decision making. Our graduates spend hundreds of hours working with students, families, and educators as part of their preparation. These "real world" experiences help future teachers to understand the lives and worlds of their students as individuals and as members of communities.

Candidates' Observations – Elementary

I believe that the Urban Institute for Teacher Education (UITE) program is one of the best in the state. I am so grateful to have a program that supports me while also challenging me. I would not change my college experience for anything. The UITE program benefits every type of learner and helps each succeed.

Elementary Education Graduate, 2017

I believe that the University of Utah and the College of Education have shaped me into becoming a critical thinking professional who seeks to teach global citizens about social justice while fostering a sense of community in the classroom.

Elementary Education Graduate, 2017

Candidates' Observations – Secondary

The Urban Institute for Teacher Education has helped support me with the best resources, the most informed professors, and the best cohort that an individual could ask for to lean on as they are going through the stress of trying to succeed in any field. It was my great honor to have been a part of the Urban Institute of Teacher Education.

Secondary Licensure Student, 2017

The Urban Institute for Teacher Education (UITE) has given me many amazing opportunities during my undergraduate education at the University of Utah. During my time, I have felt supported by the staff and my cohort leader. Truly, UITE cares and honors the education of urban youth, of which I am also a product.

Secondary Licensure Student, 2017

University of Wisconsin – Madison
Madison, WI

SCORE CARD
Elementary Indicators of Quality

Rigorous admissions process:	**A**
Learning how to teach reading:	**A**
Preparing to teach math:	**A+**
High quality practice teaching:	**D**
Learning to manage the classroom:	**F**

95% (2014-2015) **93%** (2015-2016)
GRADUATE AND GO RIGHT INTO TEACHING

What's special

Dean's Statement

The University of Wisconsin-Madison is consistently ranked as one of the finest schools of education in the United States. In turn, our graduates take this excellence into their classrooms and communities.

Our Elementary Education program is dedicated to preparing teachers who can foster high academic achievement in all students — particularly learners from diverse racial, cultural, linguistic and socioeconomic backgrounds. To accomplish these goals, our future teachers are taught how to integrate research-based practices in their teaching.

Undergraduates learn with and from fellow students as they move through our program as part of a cohort, or group, of students taking the same classes. We offer four different options that each lead to certification in two areas, including dual certification in Special Education or English as a Second Language (ESL).

Prior to graduating, students gain significant experience in local schools – with several semesters of field experience in the classroom prior to a semester of student teaching.

(continued on next page)

Where do candidates student teach?

- Madison Metropolitan School District
- Sun Prairie Area School District
- Verona Area School District

Where do graduates work?

- Madison Metropolitan School District
- Sun Prairie Area School District
- Verona Area School District

Campus Facts at a Glance

Size:	Large
Location:	City
Acceptance rate:	53%
Student to faculty ratio:	18 to 1
Graduation rate:	84%
Is education a top 5 major:	No

Financial

In-state tuition:	$10,488
Out-of-state tuition:	$32,738
In-state average annual cost:	$19,378
Students receiving federal loans:	35%
Typical debt:	$22,250
Typical Wisconsin new teacher salary:	**$33,546**

What's special about University of Wisconsin – Madison

Dean's Statement

At UW-Madison, we are committed to working actively and passionately to serve students and the community, while addressing some of society's most critical needs.

Scholarships are available specifically for our Elementary Education students.

Diana E. Hess, Ph.D.
Dean, School of Education, Karen A. Falk Distinguished Chair of Education, University of Wisconsin-Madison

Candidates' Observations

The University of Wisconsin-Madison School of Education's Elementary Education Program has challenged me to question and confront my own thoughts and biases, pushing me to be the best teacher I can be for all of my students. I am thankful to have been part of a program that has equipped me with the skills to see beyond my own experiences and recognize the individuality within a classroom.

Kayla Fritz
UW-Madison senior with the Middle Childhood-Early Adolescence/English as a Second Language cohort

The University of Wisconsin-Madison's School of Education provides the opportunity for students to have real and raw conversations that challenge you to think about relevant and real-world issues that are important in preparing you for today's world. I'm grateful to have been a part of a program that builds a strong community of pre-service teachers that I can rely on and build lifelong professional relationships with.

Morgan Johnson
UW-Madison senior with the Middle Childhood-Early Adolescence/English as a Second Language cohort

At the University of Wisconsin-Madison, I learned from a variety of passionate and well-regarded educators who empowered me to be confident in teaching students not only content and curricular matter, but also in fostering a responsive learning environment so that every child in my classroom achieves.

Sarah Morales
UW-Madison alumna and second grade teacher, Swanson Elementary, Elmbrook, Wis., School District

University of Wyoming
Laramie, WY

Outstanding
Program

SCORE CARD
Elementary Indicators of Quality

Rigorous admissions process:	A+
Learning how to teach reading:	A
Preparing to teach math:	A
High quality practice teaching:	F
Learning to manage the classroom:	A

What's special

Dean's Statement

As a graduate of the elementary education program at the University of Wyoming nearly 40 years ago, I can attest to the high-quality preparation experiences, knowledge and skills that are the continuing legacy of this program. Students in the elementary education program receive a well-rounded, up-to-date, and empirically-grounded teacher preparation program. From assessment tools to instructional strategies, from lesson planning to varied field experiences, from theory to practice, the elementary education program delivers graduates with the skills, dispositions, and knowledge to promote student achievement and develop character. Add to this our use of cutting-edge technologies such as Mursion® Augmented Reality classroom simulations, to distance clinical supervision using 360 degree cameras and ZOOM® video conferencing support, to the ATLAS® teacher video library of best teaching practices, to the Sanford Inspire® program modules and you have a 21st Century program. Finally, determining desired outcomes for this program and using of a set of common metrics such as EdTPA®, CLASS®, and other measures of graduate success and dispositions, and we can not only document our graduates' success but also scrutinize our teacher preparation programs for continuous improvements. The University of Wyoming is committed to striving for excellence in educator preparation!

Where do candidates student teach?
- Albany County District
- Laramie County School District
- Natrona County School District

Campus Facts at a Glance

Size:	Medium
Location:	Town
Acceptance rate:	95%
Student to faculty ratio:	14 to 1
Graduation rate:	55%
Is education a top 5 major:	Yes

Financial

In-state tuition:	5,055
Out-of-state tuition:	$16,215
In-state average annual cost:	$11,813
Students receiving federal loans:	36%
Typical debt:	$18,500

Typical Wyoming new teacher salary:	**$43,269**

What's special about University of Wyoming

Candidates' Observations

I would personally recommend Wyoming's Teacher Education Program for a number of reasons. Not only does Wyoming offer a variety of teacher preparation classes, but they also offer many opportunities to become prepared for life as a young professional after graduation. The experiences inside and outside of the classroom were engaging and unique. Every experience was enjoyable and practical with opportunities to tailor materials to your own individual interests. In addition to the outstanding educational experience, Wyoming offered me the opportunity to create positive relationships and connections with other students, mentors and facilitators who were there to support me along the way. Wyoming's Teacher Education Program guided me to see my potential and the amazing impact I will have as an in-service teacher. If you are looking for a phenomenal teacher program, I would highly recommend Wyoming.

Ophelia Jefferson

I would recommend this program to anyone wanting to become a teacher because the faculty and program are top notch. The college continually strives for success and to prepare the best teachers out in the field. The faculty members truly take the time to get to know you and are incredible people, who want nothing but success for every student! This program has many courses in all areas of education to make sure each and every student will be prepared for what is to come as a teacher.

Sara Richter
Student Wyoming Education Association President
College of Education Ambassadors President

The University of Wyoming has an excellent education program committed to the preparation of new teachers. The mentorship from contracted teachers who take in student teachers is strong, but even stronger are the dedicated professors who oversee the student teaching process. They are there checking on student teachers throughout the year of student teaching, giving thorough feedback during observations, and assisting the student teachers as often as needed. They are truly supportive and want to ensure success. The University of Wyoming program also offers a literacy minor that prepares graduates with a strong background in literacy going into a new teaching position.

Holly Gamroth

Western Governors University
Salt Lake City, UT

SCORE CARD

Secondary Indicators of Quality

Rigorous admissions process: **B**
Content preparation (social studies, science): **No rating/A**
High quality practice teaching: **A**
Learning to manage the classroom: **A**

71% (2014-2015) **74%** (2015-2016)
GRADUATE AND GO RIGHT INTO TEACHING

What's special

Dean's Statement

The biggest advantage of being a WGU student is the empowerment that comes with our competency-based learning model. As recent high school graduates begin at WGU, we empower them to figure out how they're going to learn the material and we help them to prove it. And so, whether they already knew it or they work to learn it, they have all the resources at their fingertips and they're in charge of how quickly they move through, when they choose to study, and how much they are going to spend.

Dr. Angie Besendorfer
*Chancellor WGU Missouri and Academic Vice President,
Teachers College, Interim*

Campus Facts at a Glance

Size: Large
Location: Suburban
Acceptance rate: N/A
Student to faculty ratio: 41 to 1
Graduation rate: 16%
Is education a top 5 major: Yes

Financial

Tuition: $6,070
In-state average annual cost: $9,862
Students receiving federal loans: 60%
Typical debt: $12,500

**Typical Utah
new teacher salary:** **$33,081**

What's special about Western Governors University

Candidates' Observations

The online platform that WGU provides allows families that have busy lives to continue to progress. Having access to my education when I was available made getting my degree possible.

Bernadette Nakamura

It helped to solidify and expand my understanding of educational principles. I was able to apply it directly to my work, as I was working!

Margaret Checchi

I was able to tailor my coursework to research and development in my employed field. I LOVED the mentor framework. My mentor was qualified, dedicated, and instructive.

Joan Runs Through

Winthrop University
Rock Hill, SC

SCORE CARD
Elementary Indicators of Quality

Rigorous admissions process:	**B**
Learning how to teach reading:	**A+**
Preparing to teach math:	**A**
High quality practice teaching:	**B**
Learning to manage the classroom:	**B**

98% (2014-2015) **98%** (2015-2016)
GRADUATE AND GO RIGHT INTO TEACHING

What's special

Dean's Statement

The teacher education program at Winthrop University is clinically-based; that is, our candidates begin in their freshman year working alongside master teachers in a variety of elementary schools. Candidates spend approximately 1,200 hours in schools throughout the program applying what they learn at the university through a "learning by doing" approach. The education core curriculum at Winthrop focuses on strategies to teach diverse learners, including children living in poverty, English language learners, students who are gifted, and students with disabilities who are included in the general classroom. In addition, field-based courses and experiences in general pedagogy (assessment, technology, and classroom climate) are developmentally sequenced and integrated with content methods. Our elementary education majors graduate with a strong background in teaching reading, math, global citizenship, and the sciences. They develop research-based strategies to meet the diverse needs of all students and connect them to the world beyond the classroom. In the senior year, candidates are placed in school within our Partnership Network to spend the entire year under the direction of a skilled mentor teacher. Teacher candidates follow the school's calendar (starting with teacher workdays in August) instead of the university's calendar for the year until graduation in May. Our teacher candidates and their mentor teachers serve as "co-teachers," promoting collaboration and shared support of student learning.

(continued on next page)

Where do candidates student teach?
- Rock Hill School Distict 3
- York County School District 1 – York
- York County School District 4 – Fort Mill

Where do graduates work?
- Rock Hill School Distict 3
- York County School District 4 – Fort Mill
- Richland County School District One

Campus Facts at a Glance

Size:	Medium
Location:	City
Acceptance rate:	69%
Student to faculty ratio:	14 to 1
Graduation rate:	53%
Is education a top 5 major:	Yes

Financial

In-state tuition:	$14,810
Out-of-state tuition:	$28,390
In-state average annual cost:	$15,760
Students receiving federal loans:	64%
Typical debt:	$27,000

**Typical South Carolina
new teacher salary:** **$32,306**

What's special about Winthrop University

Dean's Statement

The elementary education program at Winthrop University is demanding; however, our students appreciate all that they learn and the opportunity to have so much experience in schools working alongside practicing teachers. Overall, our program prepares teachers for 21st century schools.

The Elementary Education program at Winthrop University leads to South Carolina teacher licensure for grades 2-6. However, all Elementary Education majors complete all requirements to add Early Childhood Education licensure for grades PK-3, thereby providing graduates with two areas of licensure.

Candidates' Observations

Through my educational experiences at Winthrop University, I have been provided learning opportunities that I never expected. Coming to Winthrop, I thought I would simply be taught how to instruct students about general subjects like math and science; however, what I was afforded was so much more. From the very first year–very first semester, Winthrop provided me the opportunity to interact with students and use what I learned in the classroom directly in the field. I not only read books in class that taught me about the effects of poverty on students, but through my clinical experiences was able to see it first-hand. Every semester teacher candidates have that opportunity to work with children who may be gifted students, ELL students, special needs students, etc. Every student is individually unique; I truly believe that Winthrop understands that, and for that reason, sets up their curriculum accordingly. Another reason that I am grateful I chose Winthrop is the people. The professors you encounter at Winthrop are not your average professors. They know your name, they schedule meetings to see how you are doing, and they support you in any way they can. I have made many connections with wonderful people who serve as a support system for me. I go to them, trust in them, and with open arms they are willing to help me in any way they can.

This year, I have started my yearlong internship. I am so thankful for this opportunity; and having received such excellent training, I am more excited than nervous about what is to come. I am a proud believer that Winthrop is the best school I could have chosen for my major. More importantly, I am extremely confident that I will be prepared when entering the teaching field this year and in the years to come.

Ebony O. English

I feel extremely grateful to have had the opportunity to explore my degree at Winthrop because of their dedication and passion for my career choice. Not only are the professors immensely supportive of the students and their work, but the entire department motivates students to push themselves to new limits. No teacher will walk out of this education program by completing the "bare minimum" or "just getting by." When we leave this program, we are prepared for both the joys and hardships that come with the profession of teaching. With the most helpful role models, the most recent research-based practices, and hands-on experiences, Winthrop education majors are able to develop a strong sense of their individualized teaching philosophies before we enter the work force. I feel prepared and motivated to become the best teacher that I can possibly become. I would highly recommend Winthrop's education program to any individual that holds a passion in their heart to teach as they will provide an inspirational journey for all.

Savannah McJunkin

One of the many reasons I enjoy being a part of Winthrop's Elementary Education program is the amount of dedication that is seen in all aspects. Our professors show dedication through their planned coursework and activities that allow for a hands-on, minds-on experience in the classroom. They are always willing and open to shifting the way the content is seen in order to meet diverse learners. Dedication is also seen in every mentor teacher that hosts a Winthrop perspective teacher in the field placement clinicals. The partnership that Winthrop's Elementary Education program has with collaborating districts and teachers is highly respectable and is something that enriches those experiences. Attending Winthrop as a prospective teacher has enabled me to expand my thinking past my comfort zone, as well as dedicate myself to shaping future minds as the faculty, professors, and mentor teachers have shaped mine.

Rebecca Lynn Burroughs

What's special about Winthrop University

Candidates' Observations

When I decided that I wanted to be an elementary education major in high school, I immediately knew that I wanted to attend Winthrop University. Winthrop University is known for its outstanding teaching program. I knew that if I wanted to be a great teacher, I needed to attend a college or university that had a highly-qualified teaching program with knowledgeable professors who cared about me. I found all of this at Winthrop University.

My favorite thing about the teaching program at Winthrop University is the variety of courses that teacher candidates participate in. The class sizes range from 20-30 students which has allowed me to get to know my fellow colleagues and professors on a personal level. In the different courses, teacher candidates are learning about the best practices for teaching students as well as how to teach students who come from different backgrounds, cultures, and who are on different academic levels. Teacher candidates are even given the opportunity to gain hands-on experience in different classrooms at the local elementary schools to practice what they have learned. The teaching program also focuses on moving away from the "traditional" style of teaching where students are sitting at desks all day. I have learned how to implement engaging, hands-on, and student centered lessons that the students will enjoy while still meeting their educational needs and the state standards. My confidence in my teaching abilities has grown immensely since I began the teaching program at Winthrop University and it continues to grow thanks to the professors and courses that I have been offered.

Taylor Phillips

Albion College
Albion, MI

SCORE CARD

Secondary Indicators of Quality

Rigorous admissions process:	**A**
Content preparation (social studies, science):	**A**
High quality practice teaching:	**C**
Learning to manage the classroom:	**B**

Campus Facts at a Glance		Financial	
Size:	Small	Tuition:	$41,040
Location:	Town	Average annual cost:	$22,232
Acceptance rate:	72%	Students receiving federal loans:	63%
Student to faculty ratio:	12 to 1	Typical debt:	$27,200
6-year graduation rate:	69%		
Is education a top 5 major:	No	**Typical Michigan new teacher salary:**	**$35,901**

Arizona State University
Tempe, AZ

SCORE CARD

Elementary Indicators of Quality		**Secondary Indicators of Quality**	
Rigorous admissions process:	**A+**	Rigorous admissions process:	**A+**
Learning how to teach reading:	**B**	Content preparation (social studies, science):	**A**
Preparing to teach math:	**B**	High quality practice teaching:	**A**
High quality practice teaching:	**A**	Learning to manage the classroom:	**A**
Learning to manage the classroom:	**A**		

Campus Facts at a Glance		Financial	
Size:	Large	In-state tuition:	$10,370
Location:	City	Out-of-state tuition:	$26,470
Acceptance rate:	83%	In-state average annual cost:	$11,337
Student to faculty ratio:	23 to 1	Students receiving federal loans:	43%
6-year graduation rate:	64%	Typical debt:	$20,279
Is education a top 5 major:	No	**Typical Arizona new teacher salary:**	**$31,874**

Augsburg University
Minneapolis, MN

SCORE CARD
Elementary Indicators of Quality

Rigorous admissions process:	**B**
Learning how to teach reading:	**A**
Preparing to teach math:	**A**
High quality practice teaching:	**C**
Learning to manage the classroom:	**B**

Campus Facts at a Glance		Financial	
Size:	Medium	Tuition:	$36,415
Location:	City	Average annual cost:	$23,536
Acceptance rate:	45%	Students receiving federal loans:	68%
Student to faculty ratio:	13 to 1	Typical debt:	$27,000
Graduation rate:	59%		
Is education a top 5 major:	Yes	**Typical Minnesota new teacher salary:**	**$34,505**

Boston College
Chestnut Hill, MA

SCORE CARD
Secondary Indicators of Quality

Rigorous admissions process:	**A+**
Content preparation (social studies, science):	**A**
High quality practice teaching:	**D**
Learning to manage the classroom:	**B**

Campus Facts at a Glance		Financial	
Size:	Medium	Tuition:	$51,296
Location:	City	Average annual cost:	$33,661
Acceptance rate:	31%	Students receiving federal loans:	38%
Student to faculty ratio:	14 to 1	Typical debt:	$19,000
Graduation rate:	92%		
Is education a top 5 major:	No	**Typical Massachusetts new teacher salary:**	**$40,600**

Capital University
Columbus, OH

SCORE CARD

Elementary Indicators of Quality

Rigorous admissions process:	**A**
Learning how to teach reading:	**D**
Preparing to teach math:	**A**
High quality practice teaching:	**C**
Learning to manage the classroom:	**B**

Campus Facts at a Glance		Financial	
Size:	Medium	In-state tuition:	$33,492
Location:	Suburban	Average annual cost:	$22,092
Acceptance rate:	69%	Students receiving federal loans:	70%
Student to faculty ratio:	12 to 1	Typical debt:	$27,000
Graduation rate:	61%		
Is education a top 5 major:	Yes	**Typical Ohio new teacher salary:**	**$33,096**

College of Saint Benedict and Saint John's University
Saint Joseph, MN

Outstanding Program

SCORE CARD

Secondary Indicators of Quality

Rigorous admissions process:	**A+**
Content preparation (social studies, science):	**A**
High quality practice teaching:	**C**
Learning to manage the classroom:	**C**

Campus Facts at a Glance		Financial	
Size:	Small	In-state tuition:	$42,271
Location:	Suburban	Average annual cost:	$23,305
Acceptance rate:	88%	Students receiving federal loans:	65%
Student to faculty ratio:	12 to 1	Typical debt:	$26,343
Graduation rate:	83%		
Is education a top 5 major:	No	**Typical Minnesota new teacher salary:**	**$34,505**

Colorado State University
Fort Collins, CO

SCORE CARD
Secondary Indicators of Quality

Rigorous admissions process:	**A**
Content preparation (social studies, science):	**A**
High quality practice teaching:	**D**
Learning to manage the classroom:	**C**

Campus Facts at a Glance		Financial	
Size:	Large	In-state tuition:	$11,052
Location:	City	Out-of-state tuition:	$28,346
Acceptance rate:	78%	In-state average annual cost:	$16,777
Student to faculty ratio:	18 to 1	Students receiving federal loans:	45%
Graduation rate:	66%	Typical debt:	$21,004
Is education a top 5 major:	No	**Typical Colorado new teacher salary:**	**$32,126**

Concordia University Wisconsin
Mequon, WI

SCORE CARD
Secondary Indicators of Quality

Rigorous admissions process:	**B**
Content preparation (social studies, science):	**A**
High quality practice teaching:	**A**
Learning to manage the classroom:	**C**

Campus Facts at a Glance		Financial	
Size:	Medium	Tuition:	$27,900
Location:	Suburban	Average annual cost:	$23,790
Acceptance rate:	63%	Students receiving federal loans:	66%
Student to faculty ratio:	11 to 1	Typical debt:	$23,925
Graduation rate:	59%		
Is education a top 5 major:	Yes	**Typical Wisconsin new teacher salary:**	**$33,546**

Eastern Illinois University
Charleston, IL

SCORE CARD
Elementary Indicators of Quality

Rigorous admissions process: **B**
Learning how to teach reading: **A**
Preparing to teach math: **B**
High quality practice teaching: **D**
Learning to manage the classroom: **A**

Campus Facts at a Glance		Financial	
Size:	Medium	In-state tuition:	$11,580
Location:	Town	Out-of-state tuition:	$13,740
Acceptance rate:	47%	In-state average annual cost:	$16,174
Student to faculty ratio:	14 to 1	Students receiving federal loans:	66%
Graduation rate:	59%	Typical debt:	$23,650
Is education a top 5 major:	Yes	**Typical Illinois new teacher salary:**	**$37,166**

Faith Baptist Bible College and Theological Seminary
Ankeny, IA

SCORE CARD
Elementary Indicators of Quality

Rigorous admissions process: **B**
Learning how to teach reading: **A**
Preparing to teach math: **F**
High quality practice teaching: **A**
Learning to manage the classroom: **B**

Campus Facts at a Glance		Financial	
Size:	Small	Tuition:	$16,766
Location:	Suburban	Average annual cost:	$13,261
Acceptance rate:	66%	Students receiving federal loans:	37%
Student to faculty ratio:	11 to 1	Typical debt:	$15,830
Graduation rate:	65%		
Is education a top 5 major:	Yes	**Typical Iowa new teacher salary:**	**$33,226**

Furman University
Greenville, SC

SCORE CARD

Secondary Indicators of Quality

Rigorous admissions process:	**A**
Content preparation (social studies, science):	**A**
High quality practice teaching:	**D**
Learning to manage the classroom:	**A**

Campus Facts at a Glance		Financial	
Size:	Medium	Tuition:	$47,164
Location:	Suburban	Average annual cost:	$26,714
Acceptance rate:	68%	Students receiving federal loans:	31%
Student to faculty ratio:	11 to 1	Typical debt:	$25,444
Graduation rate:	84%		
Is education a top 5 major:	No	**Typical South Carolina new teacher salary:**	**$32,306**

Goshen College
Goshen, IN

Outstanding Program

SCORE CARD
Secondary Indicators of Quality

Rigorous admissions process:	**A+**
Content preparation (social studies, science):	**A**
High quality practice teaching:	**D**
Learning to manage the classroom:	**A**

Campus Facts at a Glance		Financial	
Size:	Small	Tuition:	$33,200
Location:	City	Average annual cost:	$17,533
Acceptance rate:	62%	Students receiving federal loans:	53%
Student to faculty ratio:	10 to 1	Typical debt:	$20,102
Graduation rate:	69%		
Is education a top 5 major:	Yes	**Typical Indiana new teacher salary:**	**$34,696**

Grand View University
Des Moines, IA

SCORE CARD
Elementary Indicators of Quality

Rigorous admissions process:	**C**
Learning how to teach reading:	**A**
Preparing to teach math:	**A**
High quality practice teaching:	**A**
Learning to manage the classroom:	**Not reviewed**

Campus Facts at a Glance		Financial	
Size:	Small	Tuition:	$25,474
Location:	City	Average annual cost:	$17,251
Acceptance rate:	97%	Students receiving federal loans:	77%
Student to faculty ratio:	13 to 1	Typical debt:	$23,909
Graduation rate:	47%		
Is education a top 5 major:	Yes	**Typical Iowa new teacher salary:**	**$33,226**

Grove City College
Grove City, PA

SCORE CARD
Secondary Indicators of Quality

Rigorous admissions process:	**A+**
Content preparation (social studies, science):	**A**
High quality practice teaching:	**C**
Learning to manage the classroom:	**D**

Campus Facts at a Glance		Financial	
Size:	No info	Tuition:	$ 16,630
Location:	No info	Average annual cost:	No info
Acceptance rate:	82%	Students receiving federal loans:	No info
Student to faculty ratio:	13 to 1	Typical debt:	No info
Graduation rate:	No info		
Is education a top 5 major:	No Info	**Typical Pennsylvania new teacher salary:**	**$41,901**

Harding University
Searcy, AR

SCORE CARD

Elementary Indicators of Quality

Rigorous admissions process:	A
Learning how to teach reading:	A
Preparing to teach math:	D
High quality practice teaching:	C
Learning to manage the classroom:	B

Secondary Indicators of Quality

Rigorous admissions process:	A
Content preparation (social studies):	B
Content preparation (science):	A
High quality practice teaching:	C
Learning to manage the classroom:	B

Campus Facts at a Glance

Size:	Medium
Location:	Town
Acceptance rate:	70%
Student to faculty ratio:	16 to 1
Graduation rate:	63%
Is education a top 5 major:	Yes

Financial

Tuition:	$18,635
Average annual cost:	$17,276
Students receiving federal loans:	56%
Typical debt:	$27,000
Typical Arkansas new teacher salary:	**$32,691**

Indiana Wesleyan University
Marion, IN

SCORE CARD

Secondary Indicators of Quality

Rigorous admissions process:	B
Content preparation (social studies, science):	A
High quality practice teaching:	C
Learning to manage the classroom:	A

Campus Facts at a Glance

Size:	Medium
Location:	Town
Acceptance rate:	74%
Student to faculty ratio:	14 to 1
Graduation rate:	61%
Is education a top 5 major:	Yes

Financial

Tuition:	$25,346
Average annual cost:	$26,318
Students receiving federal loans:	69%
Typical debt:	$24,104
Typical Indiana new teacher salary:	**$34,696**

Iowa State University

Ames, IA

SCORE CARD

Elementary Indicators of Quality		Secondary Indicators of Quality	
Rigorous admissions process:	A	Rigorous admissions process:	A
Learning how to teach reading:	C	Content preparation (social studies, science):	A
Preparing to teach math:	A+	High quality practice teaching:	C
High quality practice teaching:	C	Learning to manage the classroom:	D
Learning to manage the classroom:	D		

Campus Facts at a Glance		Financial	
Size:	Large	In-state tuition:	$8,219
Location:	City	Out-of-state tuition:	$21,583
Acceptance rate:	87%	In-state average annual cost:	$13,997
Student to faculty ratio:	19 to 1	Students receiving federal loans:	52%
Graduation rate:	70%	Typical debt:	$23,868
Is education a top 5 major:	Yes	**Typical Iowa new teacher salary:**	**$33,226**

Lake Superior State University

Sault Ste. Marie, MI

Outstanding Program

SCORE CARD

Elementary Indicators of Quality	
Rigorous admissions process:	B
Learning how to teach reading:	A
Preparing to teach math:	A
High quality practice teaching:	D
Learning to manage the classroom:	F

Campus Facts at a Glance		Financial	
Size:	Medium	Tuition:	$11,019
Location:	Town	Average annual cost:	$10,318
Acceptance rate:	91%	Students receiving federal loans:	57%
Student to faculty ratio:	16 to 1	Typical debt:	$23,250
Graduation rate:	43%		
Is education a top 5 major:	No	**Typical Michigan new teacher salary:**	**$35,901**

Lee University
Cleveland, TN

SCORE CARD
Elementary Indicators of Quality

Rigorous admissions process:	**A+**
Learning how to teach reading:	**C**
Preparing to teach math:	**B**
High quality practice teaching:	**C**
Learning to manage the classroom:	**Not reviewed**

Campus Facts at a Glance		Financial	
Size:	Medium	Tuition:	$15,770
Location:	City	Average annual cost:	$19,246
Acceptance rate:	87%	Students receiving federal loans:	64%
Student to faculty ratio:	17 to 1	Typical debt:	$27,000
Graduation rate:	53%		
Is education a top 5 major:	Yes	**Typical Tennessee new teacher salary:**	**$34,098**

Longwood University
Farmville, VA

SCORE CARD
Elementary Indicators of Quality

Rigorous admissions process:	**C**
Learning how to teach reading:	**A**
Preparing to teach math:	**B**
High quality practice teaching:	**C**
Learning to manage the classroom:	**C**

Campus Facts at a Glance		Financial	
Size:	Medium	In-state tuition:	$12,240
Location:	Town	Out-of-state tuition:	$27,138
Acceptance rate:	74%	In-state average annual cost:	$19,650
Student to faculty ratio:	16 to 1	Students receiving federal loans:	54%
Graduation rate:	66%	Typical debt:	$25,000
Is education a top 5 major:	No	**Typical Virginia new teacher salary:**	**$37,848**

Louisiana State University – Alexandria

Alexandria, LA

SCORE CARD
Elementary Indicators of Quality

Rigorous admissions process:	**C**
Learning how to teach reading:	**A**
Preparing to teach math:	**A**
High quality practice teaching:	**A**
Learning to manage the classroom:	**Not reviewed**

Campus Facts at a Glance		Financial	
Size:	Medium	In-state tuition:	$6,668
Location:	Rural	Out-of-state tuition:	$13,934
Acceptance rate:	33%	In-state average annual cost:	$7,370
Student to faculty ratio:	19 to 1	Students receiving federal loans:	43%
Graduation rate:	23%	Typical debt:	$17,708
Is education a top 5 major:	Yes	**Typical Louisiana new teacher salary:**	**$38,655**

Louisiana State University and Agricultural & Mechanical College

Baton Rouge, LA

Outstanding Program

SCORE CARD
Elementary Indicators of Quality

Rigorous admissions process:	**A**
Learning how to teach reading:	**A**
Preparing to teach math:	**A**
High quality practice teaching:	**F**
Learning to manage the classroom:	**A**

Campus Facts at a Glance		Financial	
Size:	Large	In-state tuition:	$10,814
Location:	City	Out-of-state tuition:	$27,491
Acceptance rate:	76%	In-state average annual cost:	$11,355
Student to faculty ratio:	22 to 1	Students receiving federal loans:	30%
Graduation rate:	67%	Typical debt:	$20,900
Is education a top 5 major:	Yes	**Typical Louisiana new teacher salary:**	**$38,655**

Maryville University of St. Louis
St. Louis, MO

SCORE CARD
Secondary Indicators of Quality

Rigorous admissions process:	**A+**
Content preparation (social studies, science):	**A**
High quality practice teaching:	**D**
Learning to manage the classroom:	**C**

Campus Facts at a Glance

Size:	Medium
Location:	Suburban
Acceptance rate:	93%
Student to faculty ratio:	13 to 1
Graduation rate:	69%
Is education a top 5 major:	No

Financial

Tuition:	$27,958
Average annual cost:	$24,484
Students receiving federal loans:	64%
Typical debt:	$23,675
Typical Missouri new teacher salary:	**$30,064**

Messiah College
Mechanicsburg, PA

Outstanding Program

SCORE CARD
Secondary Indicators of Quality

Rigorous admissions process:	**A+**
Content preparation (social studies, science):	**A**
High quality practice teaching:	**C**
Learning to manage the classroom:	**B**

Campus Facts at a Glance

Size:	Medium
Location:	Suburban
Acceptance rate:	80%
Student to faculty ratio:	13 to 1
Graduation rate:	78%
Is education a top 5 major:	Yes

Financial

Tuition:	$33,180
Average annual cost:	$25,822
Students receiving federal loans:	64%
Typical debt:	$25,989
Typical Pennsylvania new teacher salary:	**$41,901**

Miami University of Ohio

Oxford, OH

SCORE CARD

Elementary Indicators of Quality

Rigorous admissions process:	**A+**
Learning how to teach reading:	**C**
Preparing to teach math:	**A**
High quality practice teaching:	**C**
Learning to manage the classroom:	**A**

Secondary Indicators of Quality

Rigorous admissions process:	**A+**
Content preparation (social studies):	**B**
Content preparation (science):	**A**
High quality practice teaching:	**C**
Learning to manage the classroom:	**A**

Campus Facts at a Glance

Size:	Large
Location:	Town
Acceptance rate:	65%
Student to faculty ratio:	15 to 1
Graduation rate:	79%
Is education a top 5 major:	Yes

Financial

In-state tuition:	$14,736
Out-of-state tuition:	$32,555
In-state average annual cost:	$22,011
Students receiving federal loans:	38%
Typical debt:	$24,750
Typical Ohio new teacher salary:	**$33,096**

Michigan State University

East Lansing, MI

SCORE CARD

Secondary Indicators of Quality

Rigorous admissions process:	**A+**
Content preparation (social studies, science):	**A**
High quality practice teaching:	**C**
Learning to manage the classroom:	**F**

Campus Facts at a Glance

Size:	Large
Location:	City
Acceptance rate:	66%
Student to faculty ratio:	17 to 1
Graduation rate:	78%
Is education a top 5 major:	No

Financial

In-state tuition:	$14,062
Out-of-state tuition:	$37,890
In-state average annual cost:	$16,788
Students receiving federal loans:	45%
Typical debt:	$25,485
Typical Michigan new teacher salary:	**$35,901**

Minnesota State University – Mankato
Mankato, MN

SCORE CARD
Elementary Indicators of Quality

Rigorous admissions process: **B**
Learning how to teach reading: **A**
Preparing to teach math: **A**
High quality practice teaching: **C**
Learning to manage the classroom: **B**

Campus Facts at a Glance
Size:	Medium
Location:	City
Acceptance rate:	62%
Student to faculty ratio:	23 to 1
Graduation rate:	50%
Is education a top 5 major:	No

Financial
In-state tuition:	$7,858
Out-of-state tuition:	$15,602
In-state average annual cost:	$15,178
Students receiving federal loans:	58%
Typical debt:	$22,576
Typical Minnesota new teacher salary:	**$34,505**

Mount Mercy University
Cedar Rapids, IA

SCORE CARD
Secondary Indicators of Quality

Rigorous admissions process: **B**
Content preparation (social studies, science): **A**
High quality practice teaching: **A**
Learning to manage the classroom: **Not reviewed**

Campus Facts at a Glance
Size:	Small
Location:	City
Acceptance rate:	62%
Student to faculty ratio:	14 to 1
Graduation rate:	68%
Is education a top 5 major:	Yes

Financial
Tuition:	$29,696
Average annual cost:	$18,102
Students receiving federal loans:	75%
Typical debt:	$22,250
Typical Iowa new teacher salary:	**$33,226**

Nicholls State University
Thibodaux, LA

SCORE CARD
Elementary Indicators of Quality

Rigorous admissions process:	**C**
Learning how to teach reading:	**A+**
Preparing to teach math:	**A**
High quality practice teaching:	**B**
Learning to manage the classroom:	**C**

Campus Facts at a Glance		Financial	
Size:	Medium	In-state tuition:	$7,641
Location:	City	Out-of-state tuition:	$18,572
Acceptance rate:	83%	In-state average annual cost:	$10,625
Student to faculty ratio:	20 to 1	Students receiving federal loans:	49%
Graduation rate:	42%	Typical debt:	$19,848
Is education a top 5 major:	No	**Typical Louisiana new teacher salary:**	**$38,655**

North Dakota State University
Fargo, ND

SCORE CARD
Secondary Indicators of Quality

Rigorous admissions process:	**B**
Content preparation (social studies, science):	**A**
High quality practice teaching:	**B**
Learning to manage the classroom:	**D**

Campus Facts at a Glance		Financial	
Size:	Medium	In-state tuition:	$8,327
Location:	City	Out-of-state tuition:	$19,891
Acceptance rate:	93%	In-state average annual cost:	$15,139
Student to faculty ratio:	19 to 1	Students receiving federal loans:	53%
Graduation rate:	55%	Typical debt:	$23,300
Is education a top 5 major:	No	**Typical North Dakota new teacher salary:**	**$32,019**

Northwestern State University of Louisiana
Natchitoches, LA

SCORE CARD
Elementary Indicators of Quality

Rigorous admissions process:	**C**
Learning how to teach reading:	**A**
Preparing to teach math:	**B**
High quality practice teaching:	**A**
Learning to manage the classroom:	**A**

Campus Facts at a Glance		Financial	
Size:	Medium	In-state tuition:	$7,620
Location:	Town	Out-of-state tuition:	$18,408
Acceptance rate:	62%	In-state average annual cost:	$9,966
Student to faculty ratio:	20 to 1	Students receiving federal loans:	49%
Graduation rate:	38%	Typical debt:	$21,531
Is education a top 5 major:	No	**Typical Louisiana new teacher salary:**	**$38,655**

Ohio Wesleyan University
Delaware, OH

SCORE CARD

Elementary Indicators of Quality		**Secondary Indicators of Quality**	
Rigorous admissions process:	**A**	Rigorous admissions process:	**A**
Learning how to teach reading:	**A**	Content preparation (social studies, science):	**A**
Preparing to teach math:	**F**	High quality practice teaching:	**A**
High quality practice teaching:	**A**	Learning to manage the classroom:	**C**
Learning to manage the classroom:	**C**		

Campus Facts at a Glance		Financial	
Size:	Small	Tuition:	$44,090
Location:	Suburban	Average annual cost:	$28,002
Acceptance rate:	72%	Students receiving federal loans:	62%
Student to faculty ratio:	10 to 1	Typical debt:	$27,000
Graduation rate:	68%		
Is education a top 5 major:	No	**Typical Ohio new teacher salary:**	**$33,096**

Rockhurst University
Kansas City, MO

SCORE CARD
Secondary Indicators of Quality

Rigorous admissions process:	**A+**
Content preparation (social studies, science):	**A**
High quality practice teaching:	**C**
Learning to manage the classroom:	**F**

Campus Facts at a Glance		Financial	
Size:	Small	Tuition:	$35,670
Location:	City	Average annual cost:	$22,830
Acceptance rate:	74%	Students receiving federal loans:	44%
Student to faculty ratio:	11 to 1	Typical debt:	$20,500
Graduation rate:	70%		
Is education a top 5 major:	No	**Typical Missouri new teacher salary:**	**$30,064**

Seton Hall University
South Orange, NJ

Outstanding Program

SCORE CARD
Secondary Indicators of Quality

Rigorous admissions process:	**A+**
Content preparation (social studies, science):	**A**
High quality practice teaching:	**C**
Learning to manage the classroom:	**C**

Campus Facts at a Glance		Financial	
Size:	Medium	Tuition:	$39,258
Location:	Suburban	Average annual cost:	$27,199
Acceptance rate:	67%	Students receiving federal loans:	57%
Student to faculty ratio:	13 to 1	Typical debt:	$25,000
Graduation rate:	65%		
Is education a top 5 major:	No	**Typical New Jersey new teacher salary:**	**$48,631**

Spring Arbor University
Spring Arbor, MI

SCORE CARD
Secondary Indicators of Quality

Rigorous admissions process:	**A**
Content preparation (social studies, science):	**A**
High quality practice teaching:	**D**
Learning to manage the classroom:	**A**

Campus Facts at a Glance

		Financial	
Size:	Medium	Tuition:	$26,730
Location:	Suburban	Average annual cost:	$18,156
Acceptance rate:	71%	Students receiving federal loans:	75%
Student to faculty ratio:	12 to 1	Typical debt:	$24,043
Graduation rate:	53%		
Is education a top 5 major:	Yes	**Typical Michigan new teacher salary:**	**$35,901**

St. Ambrose University
Davenport, IA

Outstanding Program

SCORE CARD

Elementary Indicators of Quality

		Secondary Indicators of Quality	
Rigorous admissions process:	**A**	Rigorous admissions process:	**A**
Learning how to teach reading:	**D**	Content preparation (social studies, science):	**A**
Preparing to teach math:	**A**	High quality practice teaching:	**A**
High quality practice teaching:	**A**	Learning to manage the classroom:	**Not reviewed**
Learning to manage the classroom:	**Not reviewed**		

Campus Facts at a Glance

		Financial	
Size:	Medium	Tuition:	$29,150
Location:	City	Average annual cost:	$24,479
Acceptance rate:	64%	Students receiving federal loans:	68%
Student to faculty ratio:	11 to 1	Typical debt:	$25,764
Graduation rate:	60%		
Is education a top 5 major:	Yes	**Typical Iowa new teacher salary:**	**$33,226**

St. Louis University
St. Louis, MO

SCORE CARD
Secondary Indicators of Quality

Rigorous admissions process:	**A+**
Content preparation (social studies, science):	**A**
High quality practice teaching:	**D**
Learning to manage the classroom:	**B**

Campus Facts at a Glance		Financial	
Size:	Medium	Tuition:	$40,726
Location:	City	Average annual cost:	$31,005
Acceptance rate:	65%	Students receiving federal loans:	33%
Student to faculty ratio:	9 to 1	Typical debt:	$26,000
Graduation rate:	72%		
Is education a top 5 major:	No	**Typical Missouri new teacher salary:**	**$30,064**

St. Olaf College
Northfield, MN

Outstanding Program

SCORE CARD
Secondary Indicators of Quality

Rigorous admissions process:	**A+**
Content preparation (social studies, science):	**A**
High quality practice teaching:	**C**
Learning to manage the classroom:	**B**

Campus Facts at a Glance		Financial	
Size:	Medium	Tuition:	$44,180
Location:	Town	Average annual cost:	$23,452
Acceptance rate:	45%	Students receiving federal loans:	49%
Student to faculty ratio:	12 to 1	Typical debt:	$27,000
Graduation rate:	88%		
Is education a top 5 major:	No	**Typical Minnesota new teacher salary:**	**$34,505**

SUNY at Fredonia
Fredonia, NY

SCORE CARD
Elementary Indicators of Quality

Rigorous admissions process:	**B**
Learning how to teach reading:	**A**
Preparing to teach math:	**B**
High quality practice teaching:	**B**
Learning to manage the classroom:	**Not reviewed**

Campus Facts at a Glance

		Financial	
Size:	Medium	In-state tuition:	$8,089
Location:	Town	Out-of-state tuition:	$17,939
Acceptance rate:	62%	In-state average annual cost:	$17,220
Student to faculty ratio:	14 to 1	Students receiving federal loans:	72%
Graduation rate:	66%	Typical debt:	$25,000
Is education a top 5 major:	Yes	**Typical New York new teacher salary:**	**$43,839**

SUNY at New Paltz
New Paltz, NY

Outstanding Program

SCORE CARD
Elementary Indicators of Quality

Rigorous admissions process:	**A**
Learning how to teach reading:	**B**
Preparing to teach math:	**A**
High quality practice teaching:	**C**
Learning to manage the classroom:	**C**

Campus Facts at a Glance

		Financial	
Size:	Medium	In-state tuition:	$7,754
Location:	Suburban	Out-of-state tuition:	$17,604
Acceptance rate:	43%	In-state average annual cost:	$16,599
Student to faculty ratio:	15 to 1	Students receiving federal loans:	54%
Graduation rate:	73%	Typical debt:	$19,000
Is education a top 5 major:	Yes	**Typical New York new teacher salary:**	**$43,839**

SUNY College at Oneonta
Oneonta, NY

SCORE CARD
Secondary Indicators of Quality
Rigorous admissions process:	A
Content preparation (social studies, science):	A
High quality practice teaching:	C
Learning to manage the classroom:	D

Campus Facts at a Glance
		Financial	
Size:	Medium	In-state tuition:	$7,932
Location:	Town	Out-of-state tuition:	$17,782
Acceptance rate:	53%	In-state average annual cost:	$17,829
Student to faculty ratio:	19 to 1	Students receiving federal loans:	62%
Graduation rate:	73%	Typical debt:	$21,500
Is education a top 5 major:	Yes	**Typical New York new teacher salary:**	**$43,839**

Taylor University
Upland, IN

Outstanding Program

SCORE CARD
Elementary Indicators of Quality		Secondary Indicators of Quality	
Rigorous admissions process:	A	Rigorous admissions process:	A
Learning how to teach reading:	A+	Content preparation (social studies, science):	A
Preparing to teach math:	A	High quality practice teaching:	C
High quality practice teaching:	C	Learning to manage the classroom:	C
Learning to manage the classroom:	C		

Campus Facts at a Glance
		Financial	
Size:	Small	Tuition:	$31,472
Location:	Town	Average annual cost:	$25,709
Acceptance rate:	80%	Students receiving federal loans:	46%
Student to faculty ratio:	12 to 1	Typical debt:	$24,000
Graduation rate:	76%		
Is education a top 5 major:	Yes	**Typical Indiana new teacher salary:**	**$34,696**

Texas A & M University
College Station, TX

SCORE CARD
Elementary Indicators of Quality

Rigorous admissions process:	**A**
Learning how to teach reading:	**A**
Preparing to teach math:	**A**
High quality practice teaching:	**D**
Learning to manage the classroom:	**B**

Campus Facts at a Glance		Financial	
Size:	Large	In-state tuition:	$11,036
Location:	City	Out-of-state tuition:	$31,214
Acceptance rate:	67%	In-state average annual cost:	$13,426
Student to faculty ratio:	21 to 1	Students receiving federal loans:	33%
Graduation rate:	79%	Typical debt:	$18,750
Is education a top 5 major:	No	**Typical Texas new teacher salary:**	**$38,091**

Texas State University
San Marcos, TX

SCORE CARD
Elementary Indicators of Quality

Rigorous admissions process:	**B**
Learning how to teach reading:	**A**
Preparing to teach math:	**D**
High quality practice teaching:	**D**
Learning to manage the classroom:	**A**

Campus Facts at a Glance		Financial	
Size:	Large	In-state tuition:	$9,605
Location:	Suburban	Out-of-state tuition:	$21,029
Acceptance rate:	71%	In-state average annual cost:	$14,676
Student to faculty ratio:	23 to 1	Students receiving federal loans:	53%
Graduation rate:	54%	Typical debt:	$21,250
Is education a top 5 major:	No	**Typical Texas new teacher salary:**	**$38,091**

Towson University
Towson, MD

SCORE CARD
Elementary Indicators of Quality

Rigorous admissions process:	**B**
Learning how to teach reading:	**B**
Preparing to teach math:	**A**
High quality practice teaching:	**C**
Learning to manage the classroom:	**F**

Campus Facts at a Glance		Financial	
Size:	Large	In-state tuition:	$9,408
Location:	City	Out-of-state tuition:	$21,076
Acceptance rate:	74%	In-state average annual cost:	$17,516
Student to faculty ratio:	17 to 1	Students receiving federal loans:	47%
Graduation rate:	69%	Typical debt:	$17,750
Is education a top 5 major:	Yes	**Typical Maryland new teacher salary:**	**$43,235**

Trinity Christian College
Palos Heights, IL

SCORE CARD
Elementary Indicators of Quality

Rigorous admissions process:	**B**
Learning how to teach reading:	**A**
Preparing to teach math:	**D**
High quality practice teaching:	**C**
Learning to manage the classroom:	**Not reviewed**

Campus Facts at a Glance		Financial	
Size:	Small	Tuition:	$27,675
Location:	Suburban	Average annual cost:	$21,042
Acceptance rate:	70%	Students receiving federal loans:	71%
Student to faculty ratio:	11 to 1	Typical debt:	$24,555
Graduation rate:	60%		
Is education a top 5 major:	Yes	**Typical Illinois new teacher salary:**	**$37,166**

Union College
Lincoln, NE

SCORE CARD
Elementary Indicators of Quality

Rigorous admissions process:	**B**
Learning how to teach reading:	**A**
Preparing to teach math:	**F**
High quality practice teaching:	**C**
Learning to manage the classroom:	**A**

Campus Facts at a Glance		Financial	
Size:	Small	Tuition:	$22,538
Location:	City	Average annual cost:	$20,182
Acceptance rate:	64%	Students receiving federal loans:	74%
Student to faculty ratio:	11 to 1	Typical debt:	$27,000
Graduation rate:	53%		
Is education a top 5 major:	Yes	**Typical Nebraska new teacher salary:**	**$30,844**

University of Alabama in Huntsville
Huntsville, AL

Outstanding Program

SCORE CARD
Secondary Indicators of Quality

Rigorous admissions process:	**A**
Content preparation (social studies, science):	**A**
High quality practice teaching:	**C**
Learning to manage the classroom:	**B**

Campus Facts at a Glance		Financial	
Size:	Medium	In-state tuition:	$9,842
Location:	City	Out-of-state tuition:	$20,612
Acceptance rate:	76%	In-state average annual cost:	$18,661
Student to faculty ratio:	17 to 1	Students receiving federal loans:	46%
Graduation rate:	48%	Typical debt:	$23,500
Is education a top 5 major:	No	**Typical Alabama new teacher salary:**	**$36,198**

University of Arkansas
Fayetteville, AR

SCORE CARD
Elementary Indicators of Quality

Rigorous admissions process:	**A**
Learning how to teach reading:	**D**
Preparing to teach math:	**A**
High quality practice teaching:	**C**
Learning to manage the classroom:	**A**

Campus Facts at a Glance		Financial	
Size:	Large	In-state tuition:	$8,820
Location:	City	Out-of-state tuition:	$23,168
Acceptance rate:	63%	In-state average annual cost:	$14,546
Student to faculty ratio:	18 to 1	Students receiving federal loans:	40%
Graduation rate:	62%	Typical debt:	$21,500
Is education a top 5 major:	No	**Typical Arkansas new teacher salary:**	**$32,691**

University of Central Florida
Orlando, FL

SCORE CARD
Secondary Indicators of Quality

Rigorous admissions process:	**A+**
Content preparation (social studies):	**B**
Content preparation (science)	**A**
High quality practice teaching:	**C**
Learning to manage the classroom:	**F**

Campus Facts at a Glance		Financial	
Size:	Large	In-state tuition:	$6,368
Location:	Suburban	Out-of-state tuition:	$22,467
Acceptance rate:	50%	In-state average annual cost:	$14,221
Student to faculty ratio:	30 to 1	Students receiving federal loans:	44%
Graduation rate:	70%	Typical debt:	$18,271
Is education a top 5 major:	Yes	**Typical Florida new teacher salary:**	**$35,166**

University of Dayton
Dayton, OH

Outstanding
Program

SCORE CARD

Elementary Indicators of Quality

Rigorous admissions process:	A+
Learning how to teach reading:	A
Preparing to teach math:	D
High quality practice teaching:	C
Learning to manage the classroom:	A

Secondary Indicators of Quality

Rigorous admissions process:	A+
Content preparation (social studies):	B
Content preparation (science):	A
High quality practice teaching:	C
Learning to manage the classroom:	A

Campus Facts at a Glance

Size:	Medium
Location:	City
Acceptance rate:	60%
Student to faculty ratio:	15 to 1
Graduation rate:	77%
Is education a top 5 major:	Yes

Financial

Tuition:	$40,940
Average annual cost:	$27,884
Students receiving federal loans:	47%
Typical debt:	$26,000
Typical Ohio new teacher salary:	**$33,096**

University of Kansas
Lawrence, KS

Outstanding
Program

SCORE CARD

Elementary Indicators of Quality

Rigorous admissions process:	A+
Learning how to teach reading:	B
Preparing to teach math:	B
High quality practice teaching:	F
Learning to manage the classroom:	B

Campus Facts at a Glance

Size:	Large
Location:	City
Acceptance rate:	93%
Student to faculty ratio:	17 to 1
Graduation rate:	61%
Is education a top 5 major:	No

Financial

In-state tuition:	$11,455
Out-of-state tuition:	$28,239
In-state average annual cost:	$18,755
Students receiving federal loans:	45%
Typical debt:	$20,500
Typical Kansas new teacher salary:	**$33,386**

University of Minnesota – Morris
Morris, MN

SCORE CARD
Secondary Indicators of Quality

Rigorous admissions process:	**A+**
Content preparation (social studies, science):	**A**
High quality practice teaching:	**D**
Learning to manage the classroom:	**C**

Campus Facts at a Glance		Financial	
Size:	Small	In-state tuition:	$12,846
Location:	Town	Out-of-state tuition:	$14,846
Acceptance rate:	58%	In-state average annual cost:	$13,418
Student to faculty ratio:	12 to 1	Students receiving federal loans:	50%
Graduation rate:	66%	Typical debt:	$19,500
Is education a top 5 major:	No	**Typical Minnesota new teacher salary:**	**$34,505**

University of Missouri – St. Louis
St. Louis, MO

SCORE CARD
Secondary Indicators of Quality

Rigorous admissions process:	**A+**
Content preparation (social studies, science):	**A**
High quality practice teaching:	**D**
Learning to manage the classroom:	**C**

Campus Facts at a Glance		Financial	
Size:	Medium	In-state tuition:	$9,394
Location:	Suburban	Out-of-state tuition:	$24,525
Acceptance rate:	71%	In-state average annual cost:	$10,017
Student to faculty ratio:	18 to 1	Students receiving federal loans:	39%
Graduation rate:	41%	Typical debt:	$20,988
Is education a top 5 major:	Yes	**Typical Missouri new teacher salary:**	**$34,505**

University of Nebraska – Lincoln
Lincoln, NE

SCORE CARD

Elementary Indicators of Quality

Rigorous admissions process:	A+
Learning how to teach reading:	A
Preparing to teach math:	A
High quality practice teaching:	C
Learning to manage the classroom:	C

Secondary Indicators of Quality

Rigorous admissions process:	A+
Content preparation (social studies, science):	A
High quality practice teaching:	C
Learning to manage the classroom:	C

Campus Facts at a Glance

Size:	Large
Location:	City
Acceptance rate:	75%
Student to faculty ratio:	21 to 1
Graduation rate:	67%
Is education a top 5 major:	Yes

Financial

In-state tuition:	$8,537
Out-of-state tuition:	$23,058
In-state average annual cost:	$16,705
Students receiving federal loans:	40%
Typical debt:	$21,700
Typical Nebraska new teacher salary:	**$30,844**

University of Nebraska Omaha
Omaha, NE

SCORE CARD

Secondary Indicators of Quality

Rigorous admissions process:	B
Content preparation (social studies, science):	A
High quality practice teaching:	C
Learning to manage the classroom:	A

Campus Facts at a Glance

Size:	Medium
Location:	City
Acceptance rate:	86%
Student to faculty ratio:	17 to 1
Graduation rate:	46%
Is education a top 5 major:	Yes

Financial

In-state tuition:	$7,204
Out-of-state tuition:	$19,124
In-state average annual cost:	$12,505
Students receiving federal loans:	43%
Typical debt:	$19,500
Typical Nebraska new teacher salary:	**$30,844**

University of Sioux Falls
Sioux Falls, SD

SCORE CARD
Elementary Indicators of Quality

Rigorous admissions process:	**B**
Learning how to teach reading:	**C**
Preparing to teach math:	**B**
High quality practice teaching:	**D**
Learning to manage the classroom:	**C**

Campus Facts at a Glance		Financial	
Size:	Small	Tuition:	$27,160
Location:	City	Average annual cost:	$20,345
Acceptance rate:	91%	Students receiving federal loans:	71%
Student to faculty ratio:	16 to 1	Typical debt:	$22,750
Graduation rate:	54%		
Is education a top 5 major:	Yes	**Typical South Dakota new teacher salary:**	**$29,851**

University of St. Thomas
Saint Paul, MN

SCORE CARD
Secondary Indicators of Quality

Rigorous admissions process:	**A+**
Content preparation (social studies, science):	**A**
High quality practice teaching:	**C**
Learning to manage the classroom:	**Not reviewed**

Campus Facts at a Glance		Financial	
Size:	Medium	Tuition:	$39,594
Location:	City	Average annual cost:	$28,374
Acceptance rate:	83%	Students receiving federal loans:	55%
Student to faculty ratio:	14 to 1	Typical debt:	$26,000
Graduation rate:	74%		
Is education a top 5 major:	No	**Typical Minnesota new teacher salary:**	**$34,505**

University of Wisconsin – Eau Claire
Eau Claire, WI

SCORE CARD
Elementary Indicators of Quality

Rigorous admissions process:	**A**
Learning how to teach reading:	**A**
Preparing to teach math:	**B**
High quality practice teaching:	**C**
Learning to manage the classroom:	**D**

Campus Facts at a Glance

		Financial	
Size:	Medium	In-state tuition:	$8,812
Location:	City	Out-of-state tuition:	$16,385
Acceptance rate:	78%	In-state average annual cost:	$15,403
Student to faculty ratio:	22 to 1	Students receiving federal loans:	58%
Graduation rate:	66%	Typical debt:	$23,250
Is education a top 5 major:	Yes	**Typical Wisconsin new teacher salary:**	**$33,546**

University of Wisconsin – La Crosse
La Crosse, WI

Outstanding Program

SCORE CARD
Secondary Indicators of Quality

Rigorous admissions process:	**A**
Content preparation (social studies):	**B**
Content preparation (science)	**A**
High quality practice teaching:	**A**
Learning to manage the classroom:	**F**

Campus Facts at a Glance

		Financial	
Size:	Medium	In-state tuition:	$9,091
Location:	City	Out-of-state tuition:	$17,612
Acceptance rate:	74%	In-state average annual cost:	$15,292
Student to faculty ratio:	19 to 1	Students receiving federal loans:	57%
Graduation rate:	68%	Typical debt:	$23,250
Is education a top 5 major:	No	**Typical Wisconsin new teacher salary:**	**$33,546**

University of Wisconsin – Platteville
Platteville, WI

SCORE CARD

Elementary Indicators of Quality

Rigorous admissions process:	B
Learning how to teach reading:	A
Preparing to teach math:	C
High quality practice teaching:	A
Learning to manage the classroom:	B

Secondary Indicators of Quality

Rigorous admissions process:	B
Content preparation (social studies, science):	A
High quality practice teaching:	A
Learning to manage the classroom:	B

Campus Facts at a Glance

Size:	Medium
Location:	Town
Acceptance rate:	80%
Student to faculty ratio:	22 to 1
Graduation rate:	53%
Is education a top 5 major:	Yes

Financial

In-state tuition:	$7,484
Out-of-state tuition:	$15,334
In-state average annual cost:	$15,419
Students receiving federal loans:	61%
Typical debt:	$24,255
Typical Wisconsin new teacher salary:	**$33,546**

William Jewell College
Liberty, MO

SCORE CARD

Secondary Indicators of Quality

Rigorous admissions process:	A+
Content preparation (social studies, science):	A
High quality practice teaching:	C
Learning to manage the classroom:	**Not reviewed**

Campus Facts at a Glance

Size:	Small
Location:	Suburban
Acceptance rate:	51%
Student to faculty ratio:	10 to 1
Graduation rate:	61%
Is education a top 5 major:	No

Financial

Tuition:	$32,930
In-state average annual cost:	$20,788
Students receiving federal loans:	63%
Typical debt:	$25,000
Typical Missouri new teacher salary:	**$30,064**

Wilmington University
New Castle, DE

SCORE CARD
Elementary Indicators of Quality

Rigorous admissions process:	**A**
Learning how to teach reading:	**A**
Preparing to teach math:	**D**
High quality practice teaching:	**C**
Learning to manage the classroom:	**B**

Campus Facts at a Glance

Size:	Medium
Location:	Suburban
Acceptance rate:	Open Admission
Student to faculty ratio:	13 to 1
Graduation rate:	29%
Is education a top 5 major:	Yes

Financial

Tuition:	$10,670
In-state average annual cost:	$15,586
Students receiving federal loans:	47%
Typical debt:	$18,750
Typical Delaware new teacher salary:	**$39,338**

Other Resources

Other resources you might want to look into to guide your important decision.

- **College Scorecard** (https://collegescorecard.ed.gov/)

  The U.S. Department of Education publishes a treasure-trove of information on thousands of colleges and universities across the country. You can learn about the school's size, location, and characteristics of the student body. You can check (and compare) costs, debt, post-graduation average earnings,[48] and graduation rates. This will tell you a lot about the university.

- **School and District Navigator** (https://nces.ed.gov/ccd/schoolmap/)

  Another U.S. Department of Education tool, the School and District Navigator lets you enter an address and choose some basic characteristics, and it will display districts or schools within a certain distance from that address. You can use it to figure out the districts around your university and those where you think you might want to live and work. Keep in mind that most teachers tend to work close to where they are trained (especially where they student teach), so weigh location into your decision.[49]

  While you're at it, you can use rental cost data from Zillow (https://www.zillow.com/research/data/) and home purchase cost data from the Census Bureau's American Community Survey (https://factfinder.census.gov/faces/nav/jsf/pages/searchresults.xhtml?refresh=t) to see how hard it will be to put a roof over your head where you want to work.

- **Other college guides**

  There are many many of these out there, which can provide you with more details about the schools you may be interested in.

  For example, the Princeton Review can answer your dining hall and athletic facilities questions (among many other things)! (https://www.princetonreview.com/college-rankings/ranking-methodology)

Endnotes

1   Taie, S., and Goldring, R. (2017). Characteristics of Public Elementary and Secondary School Teachers in the United States: Results From the 2015–16 National Teacher and Principal Survey First Look (NCES 2017-072). U.S. Department of Education. Washington, DC: National Center for Education Statistics. Retrieved 5 February 2018 from https://nces.ed.gov/pubsearch/pubsinfo.asp?pubid=2017072. Over the last 30 years, between 60,000 to 140,000 new teachers (those who have never taught before) are hired each year. Cowan, J., Goldhaber, D., Hayes, K., & Theobald, R. (2016). Missing elements in the discussion of teacher shortages. Educational Researcher, 45(8), 460-462. However, school districts hire a total of about 300,000 teachers each year — including the 100,000 or so brand new teachers, as well as many teachers who previously worked in other school districts, or who had left teaching and then returned to the profession. Warner-Griffin, C., Noel, A., and Tadler, C. (2016). Sources of Newly Hired Teachers in the United States: Results From the Schools and Staffing Survey, 1987– 88 to 2011–12 (NCES 2016-876). U.S. Department of Education. Washington, DC: National Center for Education Statistics. Retrieved 5 February 2018 from http://nces.ed.gov/pubsearch.

2   Lortie, D. C. (2002). Schoolteacher: A sociological study. Chicago: University of Chicago Press.

3   Danielson, C. (1996). Enhancing Professional Practice: A Framework for Teaching. Alexandria, VA: Association for Supervision and Curriculum Development (ASCD). http://dvandkq.net/images/CPC/20120305%20CPC%20Ed%20cmte%20Danielson,%20C%20Enhancing%20Professional%20Practice%20-%20A%20Framework%20for%20Teaching.pdf

4   Watt, H. M., Richardson, P. W., & Wilkins, K. (2014). Profiles of professional engagement and career development aspirations among USA preservice teachers. *International Journal of Educational Research*, 65, 23-40.

5   Watt, H. M., Richardson, P. W., & Wilkins, K. (2014). Profiles of professional engagement and career development aspirations among USA preservice teachers. *International Journal of Educational Research*, 65, 23-40.

6   Scholastic and the Bill & Melinda Gates Foundation. Primary Sources: 2012, America's Teachers on the Teaching Profession. Page 13. Retrieved 26 March 2018, from http://mediaroom.scholastic.com/files/ps_fullreport.pdf

7   Taie, S., and Goldring, R. (2017). Characteristics of Public Elementary and Secondary School Teachers in the United States: Results From the 2015–16 National Teacher and Principal Survey First Look (NCES 2017-072). U.S. Department of Education. Washington, DC: National Center for Education Statistics. Retrieved 22 September 2017 from https://nces.ed.gov/pubsearch/pubsinfo.asp?pubid=2017072.; 2011-12 teacher data from: National Center for Education Statistics. (2015). Table 209.20. U.S. Department of Education. Washington, DC: National Center for Education Statistics. Retrieved 22 September 2017 from https://nces.ed.gov/programs/digest/d15/tables/dt15_209.20.asp.

8   U.S. Census Bureau, Population Division. (2014). Table 3. Projections of the Population by Sex and Selected Age Groups for the United States: 2015 to 2060 (NP2014-T3). Washington, DC: U.S. Census Bureau. Retrieved from: https://www.census.gov/data/tables/2014/demo/popproj/2014-summary-tables.html.

9   New York City Department of Education. (2017). Guide to the Online Teacher Application. Retrieved 20 March 2018 from http://teachnyc.net/assets/NYC_OnlineTeacherApplicationGuide.pdf.

10 U.S. Department of Education, National Center for Education Statistics, Common Core of Data (CCD), "Local Education Agency Universe Survey," 1979-80 through 2015-16. Retrieved 7 February 2018 from https://nces.ed.gov/ccd/pubagency.asp.

11 National Association of Charter School Authorizers. (2018). State-by-State Authorizer Data and Policy Analysis. Retrieved 20 March 2018 from http://www.qualitycharters.org/policy-research/.

12 National Association of Charter School Authorizers. (2018). State-by-State Authorizer Data and Policy Analysis. Retrieved 20 March 2018 from http://www.qualitycharters.org/policy-research/.

13 Taie, S., and Goldring, R. (2017). Characteristics of Public Elementary and Secondary Schools in the United States: Results From the 2015–16 National Teacher and Principal Survey First Look (NCES 2017-071). U.S. Department of Education. Washington, DC: National Center for Education Statistics. Retrieved 9 November 2018 from https://nces.ed.gov/pubsearch/pubsinfo.asp?pubid=2017071; Taie, S., and Goldring, R. (2017). Characteristics of Public Elementary and Secondary School Teachers in the United States: Results From the 2015–16 National Teacher and Principal Survey First Look (NCES 2017-072). U.S. Department of Education. Washington, DC: National Center for Education Statistics. Retrieved 9 November 2018 from https://nces.ed.gov/pubsearch/pubsinfo.asp?pubid=2017072.

14 U.S. Department of Education, National Center for Education Statistics. Table 208.20. Public and private elementary and secondary teachers, enrollment, pupil/teacher ratios, and new teacher hires: Selected years, fall 1955 through

fall 2025 Retrieved 19 March 2018 from https://nces.ed.gov/programs/digest/d15/tables/dt15_208.20.asp

15 US Department of Education, Office of Planning, Evaluation and Policy Development. (2016, July). The State of Racial Diversity in the Educator Workforce. Retrieved 26 July 2018 from https://www2.ed.gov/rschstat/eval/higher-ed/racial-diversity/state-racial-diversity-workforce.pdf

16 Taie, S., and Goldring, R. (2017). Characteristics of Public Elementary and Secondary School Teachers in the United States: Results From the 2015–16 National Teacher and Principal Survey First Look (NCES 2017-072). U.S. Department of Education. Washington, DC: National Center for Education Statistics. Retrieved 7 February 2018 from https://nces.ed.gov/pubsearch/pubsinfo.asp?pubid=2017072.

17 Gray, L., and Taie, S. (2015). Public School Teacher Attrition and Mobility in the First Five Years: Results From the First Through Fifth Waves of the 2007–08 Beginning Teacher Longitudinal Study (NCES 2015-337). U.S. Department of Education. Washington, DC: National Center for Education Statistics. Retrieved 7 February 2018 from http://nces.ed.gov/pubsearch.

18 Startz, D. (2016). What do teachers do when they leave teaching? The Brookings Institution. Retrieved from https://www.brookings.edu/blog/brown-center-chalkboard/2016/05/09/what-do-teachers-do-when-they-leave-teaching/

19 Miranda, L-M. (2012). Interview by S. A. de Carvalho. 15 questions with Lin-Manuel Miranda. The Harvard Crimson. Retrieved 26 July 2018 from https://www.thecrimson.com/article/2012/3/1/15-Questions-LinManuel-Miranda/

20 Percle, A. (2017). LBJ: From teacher to president [Blog post]. Retrieved 26 July 2018 from https://prologue.blogs.archives.gov/2017/03/05/lbj-from-teacher-to-president/.

21 Johnson, L.B. (1965). Johnson's Remarks on Signing the Elementary and Secondary Education Act. LBJ Presidential Library. Retrieved 26 July 2018 from http://www.lbjlibrary.org/lyndon-baines-johnson/timeline/johnsons-remarks-on-signing-the-elementary-and-secondary-education-act

22 Johnson, L. B. (1965). Interview by R. E. McKay. Excerpted in LBJ the Teacher. Humanities Texas. Retrieved 26 July 2018 from https://www.humanitiestexas.org/news/articles/lbj-teacher

23 U.S. Department of Education, National Center for Education Statistics, Schools and Staffing Survey (SASS), "Public School Teacher Data File," 1987-88 through 2011-12; "Private School Teacher Data File," 1987-88 through 2011-12; and "Charter School Teacher Data File," 1999-2000. (This table was prepared July 2013.) Retrieved from https://nces.ed.gov/surveys/sass/

24 Krieg, J. M., Theobald, R., & Goldhaber, D. (2016). A foot in the door: Exploring the role of student teaching assignments in teachers' initial job placements. Educational Evaluation and Policy Analysis, 38(2), 364-388.

25 Approximately 83 percent of teachers come from traditional teacher prep programs (U.S. Department of Education, Office of Postsecondary Education.(2016). Pathways to Teaching. Retrieved 3 March 2018 from https://title2.ed.gov/Public/46608_Final_Title_II_Infographic_Booklet_Web.pdf). And roughly a quarter of newly hired teachers come in with a graduate degree, meaning that a little more than half of teachers likely get their initial certification through an undergraduate program. (Warner-Griffin, C., Noel, A., and Tadler, C. (2016). Sources of Newly Hired Teachers in the United States: Results From the Schools and Staffing Survey, 1987– 88 to 2011–12 (NCES 2016-876). U.S. Department of Education. Washington, DC: National Center for Education Statistics. Retrieved 15 March 2018 from http://nces.ed.gov/pubsearch)

26 U.S. Department of Education, National Center for Education Statistics, 2008/12 Baccalaureate and Beyond Longitudinal Study (B&B:08/12). Trends in higher education. Trends in College Pricing: Published prices – national. Retrieved from https://nces.ed.gov/surveys/b&b/

27 College Board. (2017). Trends in higher education: Published prices - national. Retrieved 15 March 2018 from https://trends.collegeboard.org/college-pricing/figures-tables/published-prices-national#Published Charges, 2017-18.

28 Jenkins, D., & Fink, J. (2016). Tracking Transfer: New Measures of Institutional and State Effectiveness in Helping Community College Students Attain Bachelor's Degrees. Community College Research Center, Teachers College, Columbia University. Retrieved 24 October 2018 from https://ccrc.tc.columbia.edu/media/k2/attachments/tracking-transfer-institutional-state-effectiveness.pdf

29 Warner-Griffin, C., Noel, A., and Tadler, C. (2016). Sources of Newly Hired Teachers in the United States: Results From the Schools and Staffing Survey, 1987– 88 to 2011–12 (NCES 2016-876). U.S. Department of Education. Washington, DC: National Center for Education Statistics. Retrieved 15 March 2018 from http://nces.ed.gov/pubsearch

30 U.S. Department of Education, National Center for Education Statistics, Integrated Postsecondary Education Data System (IPEDS), "Fall Enrollment Survey" (IPEDS-EF:89-99); "Completions Survey" (IPEDS-C:90-99); "Institutional Characteristics Survey" (IPEDS-IC:89-99); IPEDS Fall 2000 through Fall 2014, Institutional Characteristics component; and IPEDS Spring 2001 through Spring 2015, Fall Enrollment component. (This table was prepared December 2015.) https://nces.ed.gov/programs/digest/d15/tables/dt15_330.50.asp

31 State of Texas Legislative Council, Legislative Budget Board Staff. (2013, February). Routes to Teacher Certification: Educator Preparation Programs. Retrieved from https://www.lbb.state.tx.us/Documents/Publications/Issue_Briefs/384_PE_RoutesTeacherCert.pdf

32   Program cost information was collected from the alternative route programs included in the *2018 Teacher Prep Review.* Costs were based on 2016-2017 school year data. For those programs that did not share cost information, costs were estimated using tuition data. Some school districts and programs provide grants to reduce or even eliminate costs to the candidate in exchange for a teaching commitment of typically two to three years

33   Follow the process laid out by the National Board for Professional Teaching Standards (www.nbpts.org), which requires teachers to build a comprehensive portfolio of evidence of their accomplished practice. Teachers need at least three years' of experience to sit for board certification. Some districts provide subsidies for the assessment and salary increases for teachers who earn National Board Certification.

34   Startz, R. (2010). *Profit of Education.* Santa Barbara: Praeger.

35   In 2016, the average total increase in teacher salaries in the largest districts in the country was 4 percent, including the average increase in salary due to having an additional year of experience and any increases due to other factors such as cost of living, but this varies by region and from year to year.

36   National Council on Teacher Quality. (2018, July). Teacher Contract Database. Retrieved July, 2018, from https://www.nctq.org/contract-database/

37   Answers: (1) $87,709 (2) $52,632 (3) $99,726 (4) $70,502

38   U.S. Department of Education, National Center for Education Statistics, Schools and Staffing Survey (SASS), "Private School Teacher Data File," 2011-12; and National Teacher and Principal Survey (NTPS), "Public School Teacher Data File," 2015–16. (This table was prepared November 2017.) Retrieved 26 March 2018 from https://nces.ed.gov/programs/digest/d17/tables/dt17_211.10.asp?current=yes.

39   U.S. Department of Education, National Center for Education Statistics, Schools and Staffing Survey (SASS), "Private School Teacher Data File," 2011-12; and National Teacher and Principal Survey (NTPS), "Public School Teacher Data File," 2015–16. (This table was prepared November 2017.) Retrieved 26 March 2018 from https://nces.ed.gov/programs/digest/d17/tables/dt17_211.10.asp?current=yes.

40   U.S. Department of Education, National Center for Education Statistics, Schools and Staffing Survey (SASS), "Private School Teacher Data File," 2011-12; and National Teacher and Principal Survey (NTPS), "Public School Teacher Data File," 2015–16. (This table was prepared November 2017.) Retrieved 26 March 2018 from https://nces.ed.gov/programs/digest/d17/tables/dt17_211.10.asp?current=yes.

41   National Board for Professional Teaching Standards. (2018, June). State Incentive Chart. Retrieved July, 2018, from http://www.nbpts.org/wp-content/uploads/state_incentive_chart.pdf

42   U.S. Department of Education, National Center for Education Statistics, Schools and Staffing Survey (SASS), "Public School Teacher Data File" and "Private School Teacher Data File," 2011-12. (This table was prepared May 2013.) Retrieved 26 March 2018 from https://nces.ed.gov/programs/digest/d15/tables/dt15_211.10.asp?current=yes. This includes 42 percent working additional duties for the school and 16 percent outside it during the school year, and 18 percent working for the school and 15 percent outside it during the summer.

43   U.S. Department of Education, National Center for Education Statistics, Schools and Staffing Survey (SASS), "Private School Teacher Data File," 2011-12; and National Teacher and Principal Survey (NTPS), "Public School Teacher Data File," 2015–16. (This table was prepared November 2017.) Retrieved 26 March 2018 from https://nces.ed.gov/programs/digest/d17/tables/dt17_211.10.asp?current=yes.

44   Levine, A. (September 2006). Educating school teachers (p. 39). Washington, DC: The Education Schools Project; Hope Street Group. (2016). On deck: Preparing the next generation of teachers. Washington, DC: Hope Street Group. Retrieved 13 June 2018 from https://hopestreetgroup.org/teacherprep/.

45   U.S. Department of Education, National Center for Education Statistics, Schools and Staffing Survey (SASS), "Public School Teacher Data File," 2011–12. Retrieved from https://nces.ed.gov/surveys/sass/tables/sass1112_2016003_t1s.asp and https://nces.ed.gov/surveys/sass/tables/sass1112_2016008_t1s.asp.

46   Levine, A. (September 2006). Educating school teachers (p. 39). Washington, DC: The Education Schools Project; Hope Street Group. (2016). On deck: Preparing the next generation of teachers. Washington, DC: Hope Street Group. Retrieved 13 June 2018 from https://hopestreetgroup.org/teacherprep/.

47   National Education Association. (2013). 2012-2013 Average Starting Teacher Salaries by State. Retrieved 9 November 2018 from http://web.archive.org/web/20180223032027/http://www.nea.org/home/2012-2013-average-starting-teacher-salary.html

48   Be careful! The College Scorecard average salary information is across all graduates, not just teachers. The National Education Association (NEA) published average starting teacher salaries by state here: http://www.nea.org/home/2012-2013-average-starting-teacher-salary.html. It's a bit dated, but it's indicative of where you'll be starting in your state and you should definitely keep these averages in mind when considering a university!

49   Krieg, J. M., Theobald, R., & Goldhaber, D. (2016). A foot in the door: Exploring the role of student teaching assignments in teachers' initial job placements. Educational Evaluation and Policy Analysis, 38(2), 364-388.